DISCERN+ ENGAGE

Essentials of Spiritual Warfare

by JOHN SMED

Copyright © 2026 by John F. Smed

Published by Prayer Current
106 – 1033 Haro Street
Vancouver, BC V6E 1C8 CANADA
www.prayercurrent.com

All rights reserved. No part of this publication may be reproduced, stored in a retrieval system, or transmitted in any form or by any means–electronic, mechanical, photocopy, recording, or any other–except for brief quotations in printed reviews, without the prior permission of the publisher.

Encouraging Words from Global Field Leaders

Fasten your seatbelt as a seasoned warrior takes you on a tour of the battlefield. As part of his "boot camp for warrior training," John wants you to stop being intimidated by evil... the theme of courage is on almost every page of the book. "Don't give Satan the high ground in your mind!

—Paul E. Miller, Author of *A Praying Life* and *A Praying Church*

John's prophetic tone is attached to his heartfelt passion for God, His Church, His Name, and Fame. He not only challenges, but he also offers practical answers on how to get back on track. It is a sober, Scripture filled, approach that steers us away from the "there's a demon behind every bush" on one hand, and the intellectual or theological elitism that acts as if Satan is not alive and well in this present darkness. Read it if you dare.

—Dr. Tom Wood, author of *Vital Grace: Getting Everything for Nothing*, President of Church Multiplication Ministries, Inc. Alpharetta, GA USA

Discern + Engage is a much-needed resource for the church today, especially in the global missions context. What I appreciate about this book is that its insights are based on a careful reading of Scripture and its applications flow out of many years of pastoral ministry. I highly recommend it!"

—Lloyd Kim, Coordinator, Mission to the World

Discern + Engage is so important for our times. It serves as an essential primer for believers looking to fortify their prayer life and increase their effectiveness in facing future changes to come. I consider it a must-read for anyone committed to deepening their spiritual resilience and understanding in this age.

—Michelle Pommells, Chief Strategy Officer, Chief Development Officer, Crossroads Christian Communications Inc. and YES TV

John Smed's *Discern + Engage* is packed with biblical, theological, historical, practical, and prayerful instruction. This book delivers years of careful research and reflection. It offers depth and breadth, with an urgent call for ordinary Christians to understand and recover their role in the essentials of spiritual warfare. I highly recommend it for individual and group study.

—Dr. Roger Helland, Prayer Ambassador,
Evangelical Fellowship of Canada

Let me begin by saying that it is a great book! Well done! John's book fills a gap in the study and training of spiritual warfare. Much has been written regarding the possession and oppression of individuals while paying little attention to the broad scope and scale of the work of the enemy in our churches, society, and political landscape. John's work moves Christ-followers from living as self-imposed victims to Spirit-filled victors.

—Willy Reimer, Executive Director, 78:7 Collective

Gripping! So many gems. The depth of research, reflection, and presentation, so far, embodies extensive thoughtfulness. Books of this depth and insights can only be written by those who have experienced the truths of which they write firsthand and live it out daily.

—Jacob George, Community Pastor and Prayer Coordinator,
Centre Street Church Calgary, Canada

I'm happy that *Discern + Engage* is now "in the wild"—we really need it. John Smed's thoughtful and biblical exploration of spiritual warfare lands at a kairos moment for the global Church. Take up and read; be encouraged by Christ's Light in the darkness.

—Karen Ellis, Director, The Edmiston Center for the Study of the Bible and Ethnicity at Reformed Theological Seminary in Atlanta

Discern + Engage is anointed. I read it through tears and weeping. Only a book sown with blood, sweat and tears and written by someone who went through the fire of testing and trial can have that effect.

> —Axa Carnes, Mentor and Advocate for mothers of victims of gender alteration

In an age where the realities of spiritual warfare often go unnoticed, *Discern + Engage* is a stirring reminder that we cannot ignore this crucial side of ministry. John Smed's book teaches us how to go from passively shaking our heads at news headlines to actively fighting evil.

> —Braeden Gregg, Content Coordinator, Redeemer City to City

In *Discern + Engage,* John Smed gives us an important and timely book for every follower of Jesus who feels disoriented and disempowered while navigating through the dense fog of enemy deception in our cultural moment. This book not only clears the fog but also reveals the radiant light of Christ in His word and through the Holy Spirit, offering us a narrow yet true path. It is an essential guide for discernment and engagement in our contested age."

> —Stephen Mulder, Co-Founder, Missional Labs

Discern + Engage is a timely and important resource. John helps everyday Christians confront this warfare.

> —Jerry Conner, Executive Director, Kansas City Kansas Baptist Association

In the west we have been lulled into pragmatism that ignores the spiritual forces at work, toys with prayer, and forgets our position in Christ and the victory he has accomplished. John Smed's work is an accessible, encouraging, and useful tool to help the Church advance.

—Chris Vogel, Church Planting & Vitality Coordinator, Mission to North America

Thanks for sharing weapons of battle. I have initially translated it into Chinese. It renews my identity as a prayer warrior. May the Lord lead the Chinese church leaders to understand the importance of joining this real spiritual battle.

—Pastor from China

As the director of a mission organization, we see clearly just how hard Satan fights everyday against the growth of God's kingdom. John's clear-eyed teaching from Scripture and real-world experience give the reader practical ways to engage in spiritual warfare without giving in to fear or timidity.

—Bob Osborne, Executive Director, Serge

Edgewood's opportunity to significantly impact Africa is not possible without a willingness to engage the forces of darkness undergirded with dependent prayer. John's book helped me to effectively pray for the Holy Spirit's power to accomplish our mission! This book will be a priority read for Edgewood's key leaders ministering on the field.

—Hal Farnsworth, Founder, Edgewood Ministries

I felt empowered and excited just by reading the table of contents. This is really a heavy weapon of warfare given to us by our Heavenly Father, and I am especially thankful for John's efforts in this.

—K. W., China Partnership

This book is so convicting, challenging, and encouraging. I feel awakened and called to battle. May the Lord give me great grace and determination to alert my elders, family and congregation to the spiritual fight and Christ's weapons to engage it well. Thank you, brother John.

—Kevin Smith, New City Fellowship, Chattanooga, TN

John Smed provides a practical exploration of the essentials of spiritual warfare from a "presby-costal" perspective. I resonate with the presby-costal perspective as I think most Korean-Americans do as well.

—Robert Kim, Associate Professor of Applied Theology and Church Planting at Covenant Theological Seminary

John"s writing genius is that his books on prayer are always practical and filled with amazing testimony. Not only did I feel challenged to be more engaged in spiritual warfare, but he showed us how to do it in each section. We are at war with the powers of darkness and the enemy never lets up. Often the attacks come from within by "concerned" wolves in sheep's clothing. Engagement is not an option!

South Asia Director, Equipping Leaders International

While some have made the study of the forces of evil sound more like a Harry Potter novel and an end in itself, *Discern + Engage* exudes a deep burden for the lost. As soon as I finished reading the book, my heart sent out a battle cry, "We shall pray and overcome; we will get the job done." The lessons arise from John's decades-long meticulous study of biblical spiritual warfare. Thankfully, none of the solutions offered by John Smed are mystical or unrealistic; rather, they are based on his more than fifty years of life and ministry. He merely asks that we open our eyes.

—Ebenezer Samuel, President, Serve India Ministries

John Smed takes us back to the source of the Bible. His sample prayers and testimonies lead us from abstract agreement into practical application for our times.

—Connan Kublik, Executive Director, Grace Network Canada

I wanted to reach out and bless the Lord for you and for this great book you have given me the privilege to feed from.

—Solomon Okelo, Regional Director, Edgewood Ministries, North Uganda

DEDICATION

This book is dedicated to those prayer captains whose labors God is multiplying to magnify his honor—Jim Whittle, José Enrique, Ebey Samuel, Karen and Carl Ellis, Christine Henrichs, Mark and Renee Reynolds, Kate W, David Westrum, Solomon Okello, Axa Carnes, and my coworkers at Prayer Current

DISCERN + ENGAGE: Essentials of Spiritual Warfare

Table of Contents

But solid food is for the mature, for those who have their powers of discernment trained by constant practice to distinguish good from evil. (Hebrews 5:14)

Introduction – A Book for Every Believer in Everyday Warfare xiii
Overview xv

Part I: Discern Your Enemy 1

We do not wrestle against flesh and blood, but against the rulers, against the authorities, against the cosmic powers over this present darkness…in the heavenly places. (Ephesians 6:12)

Chapter 1 – Survey the Bigger Picture: Living in a Christian Cosmology 5
Chapter 2 – Discern the Times, Tell the Times 21
Chapter 3 – Eyes Open to the Unholy Alliance 33
Chapter 4 – The Powers Behind the Powers that Be 47
Chapter 5 – What It Means to Take a Stand 57
Chapter 6 – Guard Against Fiery Darts 71

Part II: Critical Fronts to Take a Stand 85

Withstand in the evil day and having done all, to stand firm. (Ephesians 6:13)

Chapter 7 – Beware the Sanhedrin Within 87
Chapter 8 – Beware Lawlessness Without 101
Chapter 9 – Sifting: A Severe Pruning 119
Chapter 10 – Withstand Today's Idol Factory 122
Chapter 11 – Blessed in The Fellowship of His Sufferings 145

Part III: Engage for Conquest 157

Therefore take up the whole armour of God, that you may be able to withstand in the evil day. (Ephesians 6:13)

Chapter 12 – We Have First Strike Capability 159
Chapter 13 – Learn Military Prayer in this Age of Grace 167
Chapter 14 – Cultivate Holy Anger Against an Unholy Enemy 179
Chapter 15 – We are More than Conquerors 195

Conclusion 207

Appendix – How to Lead a Prayer-Book Study that Brings Transformation 211
Recommended Resources for Further Study 215

All Scripture references are from the English Standard Version unless otherwise noted.

INTRODUCTION

A Book for Every Believer in Everyday Warfare

At the time of writing, wildfires have just devastated our home city of Kelowna, in the interior of British Columbia. One hundred and eighty homes were burned to the ground and countless hectares of forest were reduced to barren spires. We had to evacuate our home, and a neighbor 500 meters away lost their home. The signs of an out-of-control forest fire are obvious: smoke, soot, gas tank explosions, red flames across the night skyline, trees and houses bursting into flame, not to mention an army of fire fighters in the air and on the ground. We experienced a surreal suspension of time as we waited helplessly for winds and weather to change. Once the flames and smoke subsided, the grief and pain of those who had lost their homes began to emerge.

There is another fire burning out of control. It is a spiritual fire enveloping our world. Everyone senses something is amiss, but discerning Christians read the signs—the godless and lawless forces gaining momentum, and the fiery darts aimed at the emerging generation. In the devastating aftermath of this spiritual inferno, we see the scorched wreckage of those who have lost their innocence by being told a lie and believing it.

No human force can tame, much less stop, this fire. However, there is a divine outpouring that can quench any fire. In answer to urgent and united prayer, God pours out his Spirit to quench the flames.

We sat by helpless while the flames devoured hectares of forest and home after home. Trained and equipped ground workers and water bombing pilots were called in to corral the fires and save the day. In the spiritual battle, trained and equipped Christians are the ground workers and water pilots called to stay the inferno. No true believer evacuates the field. As we take our stand, all the fiery darts of the evil one will be doused.

Even where the fire has had its way, all is not lost. There are sprouts of hope. Foresters tell us that a burned-over area is safe from fire for at least 30 years. A few months after the devastation, green life rises from the ashes.

The fires have raged, vast swaths of church and world are charred, yet it is not too late for the Holy Spirit to douse the flames and renew the land. We are more than conquerors through him who loves us. His presence and power await our prayers.

Overview

Part I of this book, ***Discern Your Enemy,*** focuses on the big picture.

Study Scripture and you realize spiritual warfare goes beyond engaging demonic personalities—the battle has cosmic, cultural, church, and personal fronts. The parameters of spiritual warfare are as wide as the conflict of kingdoms:

> *Giving thanks to the Father, who has qualified you to share in the inheritance of the saints of light. He has delivered us from the domain of darkness and transferred us into the kingdom of his beloved Son, in whom we have redemption, the forgiveness of sins.* (Colossians 1:12-13)

Spiritual warfare includes confronting world forces that oppose Christ and his gospel, contending for the faith against heretical teachers, as well as our battle against indwelling sin. This unseen contest is woven into every aspect of the Christian life. War is not everything, but war is a part of everything. A believer is always a soldier of the cross. We must always stand on guard. Our weapons must always be honed and ready.

If we widen our perspective to survey the cosmic arena of spiritual warfare, our awareness of the greater conflict of kingdoms can propel us to take a united stand against the enemy. Our battle is army against army. Unfortunately, this wider arena is too seldom addressed.

While our team was teaching a course on prayer at a Bible school, I asked 25 students, who met regularly to pray, if they prayed for their church. No one raised his or her hand. Then I asked if any prayed for their community or city. Again, no hands were raised. Prayer requests were confined to private and individual concerns.

Part II, *Critical Fronts to Take a Stand,* equips us to discern and withstand the world forces that tempt and torment believers everywhere. *Woe the world for temptations to sin* (Matthew 18:7). We spend time studying the apocalyptic dimensions of our conflict. This eschatological (end times) dimension of spiritual warfare is often—and catastrophically—neglected. Christians need to discern the present times in relation to the Lord's imminent return to prepare for each new phase of the enemy's strategy. *Where there is no prophetic vision, the people perish* (Proverbs 28:19).

The apostles teach that the last days will be accompanied by the intensification of Satan's activity: *The devil has come down to you in great wrath, because he knows that his time is short* (Revelation 12:12). The return of the Lord corresponds to the increasing activity of Satan and his armies (see 2 Timothy 3:1-5; 2 Thessalonians 2:1-12; 2 Peter 3:3,4; 1 John 2:18, 4:2,3; Jude 1:17-20; and Revelation, especially Chapters 12-18). The note of urgency inspires every believer. *Lift your heads, your redemption draws nigh* (Luke 12:28, NKJV).

Part III, *Engage for Conquest,* we study the front line of spiritual battle. Wherever the gospel is faithfully proclaimed is the frontline of spiritual warfare. When the apostles enter a new field, they preach to the city (Acts 8:8, 14:21). As they evangelize, Paul tells us that they are making Christ known to unseen hosts (Ephesians 3:10). Public evangelism destroys strongholds, upsets, uproots and overturns the existing order (see Acts 14:8ff, 16:20, 17:5,8, 19:29).

Missionary work, specifically evangelism, brings persecution by the world. Premeditated attacks against the church and the gospel are Satanic in origin. Believers living under persecuting powers are in a constant battle against the hosts of wickedness— and they know it. Believers endure interrogation, imprisonment and other forms of abuse and violence. This is concrete evidence of an alliance of seen and unseen powers. We will argue that the onslaught of evil against Christians is just as real in the West, though less overtly coercive or violent. Economic opportunity and prosperity blind us to unseen realities. We confuse the free market with spiritual freedom.

Near the end of each chapter a prayer will guide the reader in applying the content. Each chapter concludes with a testimony.

Throughout the book, we focus on the importance of prayer as the all-purpose instrument of our warfare and chief weapon in our arsenal for advancing against the enemy. When mystified by the nature of the opposition, pray; when overwhelmed by the onslaught, pray; to identify the enemy, pray; before you enter spiritual warfare, pray; during spiritual warfare, pray; to resist Satan, pray; after the victory, give thanks, and pray.

Having prayed, we will have done that which is essential. As Calvin wrote, "The principal work of the Spirit is faith, the principal exercise of faith is Prayer." E. Stanley Jones said, "The one who prays well has fought well."

Two Streams

In following pages, the main subject is the accelerating progress of evil in the world. Yet, I am not a pessimist but am filled with hope when it comes to the surpassing power of Christ to overcome our enemies. I am also filled with hope as I consider the promises that the message of Christ will multiply throughout the world. It belongs to the church to do more than survive. The good news will greatly advance in saving effect and transforming power. The growing darkness is Satan's retaliation against kingdom advances.

As evil progresses in its hostile intensity, the gospel flourishes in saving abundance. I will refer to astonishing numbers of conversions around the world, and the wonderful multiplication of the gospel in many lands. Consider that there were 10 million Christians in Africa in 1950. Those numbers have swelled to more than 600 million today. It is common agreement that the West has not shared in these recent advances—at least for the last half century or more. The reason for this is not complex. When sin is not confessed, or judged, it accumulates and accelerates.

Some understand biblical prophecy to indicate a tremendous advance of the gospel as we near the end. Others understand prophecy to indicate that the world will become increasingly evil and good will be almost extinguished. I will argue for both. It is the Christian end times consciousness, predicted in the Bible, that there will be a surging river of gospel advance in the last days. At the same time there will be a corresponding opposition and alliance of evil. This sets the stage for the final conflagration.

I am not attempting to present a comprehensive eschatology (view of the end times). My objective is to open eyes to discern the surrounding powers, good and bad, and to equip believers with the essentials of spiritual warfare.

There are two other streams that merge to inform our end times hope. A Christian lives within the dynamic of two different, but complementary hopes. The New Testament hope is that the Lord Jesus could return tomorrow. At the same time, we are empowered by the promise, *"Go make disciples of all nations."* The near horizon of the Lord's return is combined with the broad vista of global evangelization. As we eagerly await the second coming, we patiently and boldly obey the command by proclaiming Christ as Savior and Lord—knowing that people from every nation will be reaped in the great harvest of salvation. The combination of these two powerful truths fuels both present urgency and persevering courage.

I do advocate for the immanent return of Jesus. I can confidently assert; *Salvation is nearer now then we first believed* (Romans 13:11). I affirm the hope of the apostles, who were *waiting for and hastening the coming day of the Lord* (2 Peter 3:12). In the meantime, with diligent perseverance, we apply ourselves to our calling and task; *Blessed is that servant, whom his Lord when he comes shall find so doing* (Matthew 24:46).

Background Reading to Go Deeper

For fifty years, I have studied the Scriptures in depth on spiritual warfare. I drink deeply at the well of fathers, mothers, sisters, and brothers who "walk the talk" (at the end of the volume I have included a brief biography of thinkers who have shaped my understanding of spiritual warfare). Reformed thinkers like Jacques Ellul have shaped my thoughts concerning the political dimensions of spiritual warfare, especially in his work, *The Meaning of the City*. Several studies of the book of Revelation have been helpful, especially Dennis Johnson's *The Triumph of the Lamb*. This commentary fuels a joyous assurance for me about the ultimate power of Jesus over all the forces and strategies of the enemy, as well as aiding my understanding of the identity of the antichrist, the beast, and Babylon (Johnson's footnotes in the ESV are also hugely helpful).

I have feasted on the works of the "Anglo-costal," C.S. Lewis. I refer the reader to his enormously profitable and engaging *Space Trilogy*. Lewis considered the second volume, *Perelandra*, his favorite work. In this book Lewis gives a detailed and dramatic reenactment of the battle between Satan and our first parents in the garden. The third volume, That *Hideous Strength*, is a prophetic unmasking of the insidious influence of evil in upper echelons of education. It reverberates with chilling contemporary relevance.

If someone wants to read a good primer on spiritual warfare, I recommend Brian Zacharias's work, *The Embattled Christian*. We reserve our highest praise for John Bunyan's immortal work, *The Pilgrim's Progress*. This biblically rich allegory depicts every Christian's life as a series of spiritual battles against the world, the flesh, and the devil. It is filled with episodes of dark conflicts and exultant victories in the many trials Christian faces on his journey from the City of Destruction to the Celestial City.

Author's Notes

I tell people, "I am presby-costal." I embrace Reformed and Pentecostal Christians as members of the same family. I love the theological depth of Reformed Christians, with their focus on our struggle against sin within. As for Pentecostal Christians, I eagerly embrace their straightforward acceptance of whatever God says and their courage to obey what Christ commands. I especially love their eager willingness to endure reproach for a bold and public faith. There are many Presbyterians and not a few Pentecostals who would be happy to call themselves presby-costals.

Serving as a prayer trainer and pastor for four decades has made me realize there is a gap in resources for everyday Christians who faithfully fight the good fight. My reformed brethren have muscular theology but often lack awareness when it comes to supernatural dimensions of our conflict. My Pentecostal brethren have a strong supernatural outlook but are not always tethered to biblical foundations. Our aim is to plow a middle furrow with the sharp plowshare of Scripture, to overturn depleted conceptions, and dig deep to uncover nutrient rich teachings beneath.

These chapters are not written for exorcists, though no doubt we need them. Sensational manifestations are rare, and those who are trained to deal with them are rarer still. On the other hand, every believer must do combat with the world, the flesh, and the devil every day.

This is a biblical study for practical use for people eager to see below the surface anarchy of our times—to discern the roots and even subterranean causes beneath the present rise of evil in world. This is a book written by a soldier for fellow soldiers.

I draw insights from a life of missionary prayer. It began some fifty years ago when my wife and I were reborn in a community that believed in prayer and affirmed the opposition of Satan. L'Abri Fellowship, in the Swiss Alps, attracted a host of lost and seeking young people from around the world. Conversions abounded.

Welcomed to live alongside our hosts in one of the chalets, newcomers experienced the profound workings of the Spirit of Christ. This community was rich in prayer—at meals and studies, evenings of prayer and monthly days of prayer and fasting. The atmosphere reverberated with the same palpable grace that echoed in the early Church; *And awe came upon every soul, and many wonders and signs were being done through the apostles* (Acts 2:43).

Since then, for forty years, I have been pastor, mission leader, and active evangelist. I count myself among *those who have their powers of discernment trained by constant practice to distinguish good from evil* (Hebrews 5:14).

The best war strategists are those who are veterans of combat. The very best leaders are those who have suffered defeat as well as victory, especially when their own decisions figure in the loss! If that is the case, I belong with the best veterans. I have experienced God's plenty confronting evil in its many forms. Within my own soul, I combat remaining sin; in serving God's people I come alongside and wrestle with the lure and lies of the world; and in unashamed evangelism, I experience the opposition of the world and the devil.

Along with my wife Caron, family, and fellow soldiers, we have helped plant a mission network, a prayer ministry, and two churches—the second in Vancouver's city center. The latter has been our greatest proving ground. We have learned about the power of evil in the "mean streets" of the city. We also experienced the rising tide of evil in the "clean streets."

I recall an explicit encounter with agents of wickedness. Every year we hosted two or three open house gala events we called Art in the City / Art in the Sanctuary at our Vancouver location. This outreach featured accomplished artists and musicians. Hundreds of guests came through on a weekend. Several artists found their way into the church and into Christ through these open-door events. One evening, I went downstairs and encountered a seated circle of whirling and chanting young men and women.

One of them was a newcomer to the church who asked to be a part of organizing this Art in the City event. A lavishly dressed woman in flowing robes was orchestrating. Puzzled and a little alarmed, I asked, "What are you doing?" She replied, "We are inviting spirits to join in celebration."

I told them to leave—immediately. They left. That night I prayed with several of our church team for God to frustrate this channeler's endeavors. The next day, I sent an email to the many churches and individuals supporting our work, asking them to unite and persevere in prayer against this invasion. God rained down confusion, disrupting and smothering her work. Two weeks later, I received a letter from this woman. It was a profuse apology for crashing our event. She promised not to do it again. This is not the first or last time we have resisted the devil and watched him flee.

For more than twenty years, we have been active working in regions of the world where demonic activity is more obvious, especially Cuba, East Africa, and India. These bold Christians pray a great deal but needed training in the cosmic and Kingdom dimensions of prayer. We do not train these believers in spiritual warfare; they train us! In China, the confrontations in spiritual warfare are less manifest, but no less real. For these Christians, the most obvious antagonist is the world powers, a beast rising from the sea (Revelation 13:1). The everyday language of the Church in China is militant and filled with references to the activity of Satan. As one pastor preached, "the government has the agenda of the antichrist, and seeks to build an earthly utopia."

PART I

Discern Your Enemy

> "Alike pervaded by his eye, all parts of his dominion lie.
> The world of ours and worlds unseen,
> and thin the boundary between."
>
> —Josiah Condor, 1854

The Christian life is not all war, but there is war in every part. The battle is constant and pervasive. There can be no surrender: there is no truce. It is conquer or be conquered. Any formulation of Christian spirituality that overlooks this reality is radically deficient.

Many are blind to the all-encompassing nature of our conflict. Some imagine that spiritual warfare is limited to identifying and confronting demons, yet neglect the cosmic, cultural, and ecclesiastical dimensions of the battle.

Sooner or later, every Christian will have personal tribulations and confrontations with the enemy. Yet these battles are only one dimension of a greater, global conflict to which every angel, demon and human being has been conscripted. The destiny of individuals, cities, and nations is at stake. The church as the representative body of Jesus Christ in the world is stationed at the front line.

Despite urgent global, national, and urban concerns, today's "normal" prayer meetings focus on personal concerns of health and well-being. Rarely is a prayer meeting devoted to seeking God for truth in government, justice in the courts, temperance in the marketplace, or conscience in centers of education.

The neediest residents in our churches, cities and local communities suffer without our prayers. While we could make a difference, instead we are left frustrated and overwhelmed by the corruption, injustice, and sorrow surrounding us.

Contrast the current reality with God's promise to heal an entire nation in answer to repentant prayer. It is a humble and repentant church that brings healing to its world.

> *If my people who are called by my name will humble themselves and pray and seek my face and turn from their wicked ways, then I will hear from heaven and will forgive their sin and heal their land.* (2 Chronicles 7:14)

Or consider this exhortation to pray for the church and world:

> *First of all, [first in sequence and first in priority] I urge that supplications, prayers, intercessions, and thanksgivings be made for all people, for kings and all who are in high positions, that we may lead a peaceful and quiet life, godly and dignified in every way. This is good, and it is pleasing in the sight of God our Savior, who desires all people to be saved and to come to a knowledge of the truth.* (1 Timothy 2:1-4)

This is a call to prayer of global dimensions. Paul encourages us to pray for all people, for kings and all who are in high positions. He includes praying for domestic flourishing, that we may lead a peaceful and quiet life, godly and dignified in every way. At the same time, these requests echo the desire of God, who desires all people to be saved.

Notes from the Underground Church

As we pray, God opens eyes to see the bigger picture.

A few years ago, I met a movement leader of underground churches in China. E. W. got hold of our prayer walking materials and translated and distributed them to church leaders in China. As Christians began to take regular prayer walks in their community, he reported to me that some pastors wept and confessed: "We had stopped caring for the lost in our city." They had ignored those outside the church or even held them in contempt. As they prayed, they realized this attitude grieved the Spirit. Praying for their community opened their eyes to the spiritual lostness and misery of their neighbors. They became like Jesus, while going through the towns and villages of his day. When he saw that the crowds were harassed and helpless, like sheep without a shepherd, he had compassion on them. With renewed hope the disciples' eyes were opened to see that the field are white for harvest (Matthew 9:36-37; John 4:35).

As they prayed, these Chinese believers' hearts changed—and so did their behavior. One church group set about picking up garbage in the trash-strewn common spaces between the tall apartment buildings. Other brothers and sisters installed lighting in the stairwells of tall apartments, creating safety for women and young people who used the stairs at night. When a house church could not find enough space to gather in their neighborhood, they faced the prospect of moving. A local community council asked them; "Please stay." These house church Christians gained boldness to share Christ with their neighbors. They had learned to live out Christ's imperative: *Let your light so shine before others, so that they may see your good works and give glory to your Father who is in heaven* (Matthew 5:16).

CHAPTER 1

Survey the Bigger Picture (Living in a Christian Cosmology)

> "Even though this world with devils filled,
> should threaten to undo us,
> We will not fear for God hath willed
> his truth to triumph through us."
>
> —Martin Luther, *A Mighty Fortress is our God*

The Bible's imagery of the cosmos depicts an "above, below and in-between" realm.

> There are three worlds. One is this, which is an intermediate world—a world in which good and evil are so mixed together as to be a sure sign that this world is not to continue forever. Another is heaven, a world of love, without any hatred. And the other is hell, a world of hatred, where there is no love, which is the world to which all of you who are in a Christless state properly belong. This last is the world where God manifests his displeasure and wrath, as in heaven he manifests his love.[1]

Heaven and hell interpenetrate each other, in the realm between them. Christians live in between, in a world teeming with unseen realities. The very fabric of the cosmos is held together supernaturally. The Bible tells us that *in him all things*

---

[1] Jonathan Edwards, *Sermons*, "Heaven is a World of Love"

hold together (Colossians 1:17) and that *in him we live and move and have our being* (Acts 17:28). We are surrounded by *a cloud of witnesses* (Hebrews 12:1), and are told that multitudes of angels move between realms interacting and influencing this world: *Their angels always see the face of my Father who is in heaven* (Matthew 18:10). Evil spirits interact with the seen world and on some occasions can even appear before God in the courts of heaven, as we see in the story of Job (Job 1:6, 2:1).

This interaction of heaven, earth, and hell proves a critical principle of spiritual warfare: there is no "natural" realm devoid of unseen supernatural realities. As Elizabeth Barrett Browning wrote, "Earth is crammed with heaven." We live in a supernatural universe.

There Are Angels Among Us

The population of heaven is always on active duty. God names himself *El Gibbor*, A Mighty Warrior. He is called the "Lord of Armies" 260 times in the Bible. Angels make up the army hosts of God. Angels are mentioned 100 times in the Old Testament and 175 times New Testament. These heavenly warriors make up an army of more than a hundred million: *The chariots of God are twice 10 thousand, thousands upon thousands: the Lord is among them* (Psalm 68:17). The same number is repeated in Daniel 9:8 and Revelation 5:11. This repetition suggests the number is not just symbolic.

When angels appear in biblical history, God often assigns them to a military mission. Consider the cherubim with the flaming sword at the gates of Eden (Genesis 3:24); the three angelic beings on reconnaissance who adjudicate and execute judgment at Sodom (Genesis 18:1-19:29); or the captain angel of the Lord, who meets Joshua at Jericho (Joshua 5:13-15). Angels guard and keep God's people (Psalm 91:9-11).

Angels surround and defend the people of God. First Kings provides a dramatic illustration. Elisha is a seer, gifted with eyes to see the presence of angel warriors. When his servant Gehazi panics at the sight of the Syrian army surrounding the city, Elisha prays for God to open his eyes:

"Oh no, my lord! What shall we do?" the servant asked. "Don't be afraid," the prophet answered. "Those who are with us are more than those who are with them." And Elisha prayed, "Open his eyes, LORD, so that he may see." Then the LORD opened the servant's eyes, **and he looked and saw the hills full of horses and chariots of fire all around Elisha.**
(1 Kings 6:15-17 NIV)

Angels bring visions and revelations from the throne room of God. Michael, the prince of angels, reveals the future to Daniel after wrestling with the *Prince of Persia* (Daniel 10:13). When he sets himself to pray, Daniel is unaware that his prayers figure in the destiny of nations. After fasting and praying for 21 days, his eyes are opened by an angel to what has transpired in unseen realms:

While I was still in prayer, Gabriel, the man I had seen in the earlier vision, came to me in swift flight about the time of the evening sacrifice. He instructed me and said to me, "Daniel, I have now come to give you insight and understanding. ***As soon as you began to pray, a word went out, which I have come to tell you, for you are highly esteemed.*** (Daniel 9:21-23 NIV)

The gospels and Acts furnish numerous examples of angelic activity. Ministering angels always behold the face of God and are his agents to guard and keep children from sin and Satan: *their angels always see the face of my Father who is in heaven* (Matthew 18:10). Angels lead evangelists to sinners (Acts 8:2) and bring sinners to evangelists (Acts 10:1-8). Angels rescue gospel messengers and execute God's judgments (see Acts 12:5, 23-24). On the last day, angels will weed out the wicked and throw them into a fiery furnace (Matthew 13:41-42).

God summons mighty angels to action in answer to our prayers. Though we are seldom aware of their presence among us, Scripture teaches us that angels often visit us, perhaps daily. Billy Graham comments, "If we would only realize how close his ministering angels are, what calm assurance we could have in facing the cataclysms of life." John Calvin adds:

The Bible tells us that God has innumerable guardians to look after our safety; that so long as we are hedged about by their defense and keeping, whatever perils may threaten, we have been placed beyond all chance of evil. Angels keep vigil for our safety, take upon themselves our defense, direct our ways, and take care that some harm may not befall us… every ready to bring help to us with incredible swiftness… even as lightning sent forth from heaven flies to us with its usual speed.[2]

John Paton was a pioneer missionary to New Hebrides Islands. One night hostile natives were set to attack the missionary headquarters, but the Patons prayed to God, and the natives suddenly turned away. Paton later found out that the tribe refrained from attacking them because they saw that the headquarters was surrounded by "hundreds of men" dressed in shining garments with swords drawn.[3]

Believers have much in common with angels. Every believer is part of the Lord's standing army. Like angels, believers behold the face of God continually (2 Corinthians 3:18). Like angels, Christians are messengers, *angellos,* of the good news. Like angels, we are sent to minister to the household of God. Like angels, our prayers guard the Church and bless the nations.

On the dark side, the demons of hell are also among us. Forever on alert, they are stationed and ready. We read that a third of the stars of heaven fell in the primordial war (Revelation 12:4). We can assume the rebel camp is made up of millions of fallen angels and their allies. These devils are in constant battle with the angels of God in the heavenly realms. Conflict on earth is a part of this unseen heavenly warfare:

> *For we do not struggle against flesh and blood, but against the rulers, against the authorities, against the powers of this dark world and against the spiritual forces of evil in the heavenly realms.* (Ephesians 6:12)

Humankind is embedded between two opposing forces, every person serving one side or the other. In 1938, the world was in a state of relative peace. From 1939 to 1945 the world was in a state of war. Once war is declared between nations on earth, every citizen is instantly on the side of their nation. Allying with the other side is treason. Avoiding the duties of war is an act of cowardice. In the war between heaven and hell, the inhabitants of earth are divided into two camps, and unquestioning loyalty is required by both sides.

---

[2] Ron Rhodes, *Angels Among Us* (Nashville: Thomas Nelson, 2008), 170.
[3] Ibid, *Angels Among Us,* 179.

Personal Sanctification Is Woven into Every Dimension of Spiritual Warfare

Our enemies are the world, the flesh, and the devil. The battle against flesh is fought within. Sanctification is a war of the flesh versus the Spirit. The language of this inner conflict is military.

> *For the desires of the flesh are against the Spirit, and the desires of the Spirit are against the flesh, for these are opposed [from "opponent" or "adversary"] to each other, to keep you from doing the things you want to do.* (Galatians 5:17)

Several works have afforded biblical counsel and encouragement to many in their inner war: John Calvin's *The Golden Booklet of the Christian Life;* Andrew Murray's *Humility;* J.I. Packer's *The Pursuit of Godliness;* David McIntyre's *The Hidden Life of Prayer;* and an all-time favorite, John Bunyan's *Pilgrims Progress.*

A Christian's inner struggle against sin is rooted in the larger battle. Awakenings are a composite of thousands of revived believers. Consider the Welsh revival of 1904 and 1905. Each Christian committed to what became known as the "Four Points":

1. Confess all known sin,
2. Put aside all doubtful habits,
3. Promptly obey the Holy Spirit,
4. Make Christ known publicly.

In a few years many thousands came to Christ in Wales alone. "A hundred thousand were outsiders that were converted and added to the churches" writes revival historian J. Edwin Orr. Five years later, 75 percent were still in the church. Orr reports that the fires of revival spread to more than two million new believers worldwide. From 1903 to 1906, 300,000 people were added to the Free Churches of England. Orr adds, "In the United States the seven major denominations increased by more than two million in five years, 870,389 new communicants in 1906."[4]

---

[4] J. Edwin Orr, *The Re-study of Revival and Revivalism* (Wheaton, IL: International Awakening Press, 2000), 43–45.

The apostle Paul points out that a believer's attention to spiritual growth in holiness has eternal repercussions, for self and for others.

Set the believers an example in speech, in conduct, in love, in faith, in purity ... Practice these things, immerse yourself in them…Keep a close watch on your yourself and on the teaching. Persist in this, for by doing so you will save both yourself and your hearers (1 Timothy 4:12, 15-16).

When a Christian makes personal holiness a priority, there is a promise for others. Those who take time to be holy have power to fight the good fight and reap the harvest.

Defining the Powers in Cosmic Warfare

The continual warfare between heaven and hell is a "theomacy," a war between titanic gods. Babylonian mythology maintained that the world is built from the carcass of Tiamat, the god who was killed in a battle with the god Marduk. The contestants in the biblical cosmology are the Sovereign Omnipotent Lord versus all the false gods and idols deployed by Satan and his allies. Heaven is drawing us up. Hell is dragging us down.

There is heavenly power and there is demonic power. The powers of heaven and powers of hell are of an entirely different order.

1. Heaven's power is infinite and sovereign. Satan's power is limited and subordinate. Scripture says *power belongs to God* (Psalm 62:11). If anyone has power, even Satan, it is only by God's permission.

2. God's power is just holy and good. The devil's power is hateful and cruel.

3. Heaven's power is regenerative. The enemy's power is destructive. God's power is resurrection power. Satan has one intent: to destroy and mar what God has created.

4. Our Lord's power is victorious. When Jesus surrendered his life at the cross, Satan was crippled and disarmed. He is a defeated enemy who knows his time is short.

The cosmic contest between good and evil is not a battle of equals. Jesus *cast out the spirits with a word* (Matthew 8:16). The captain of heaven's forces is the Lord of the cosmos—he is the King of all creation and Lord of all redemption.

Jesus Has Already Won the Decisive Battle

Satan cannot contest with God—he is under God's power and reign like any created being. He wages war with his demon army against angel and human agents. Satan has a counterpart. Michael is the general of heaven's armies. In this internecine battle, Satan is both outnumbered (see Revelations 2:4) and outpowered (Jude 9). Michael and his angels are more powerful than demons because they are not weakened by wickedness. Do not be afraid. When God's people cry out with all their hearts, God sends his angel army to defend us, deliver us, and defeat our foes.

Jesus' birth, life, death, and resurrection is the epicenter of a war of the worlds that reverberates to the final conflagration.

The birth of Jesus represents a military invasion into enemy territory. Jesus was sent by God on a military mission. Consider the original Salvation Army Choir that attends the birth of Christ:

And there were shepherds living out in the fields nearby, keeping watch over their flocks at night. An angel of the Lord appeared to them, and the glory of the Lord shone around them, and they were terrified. **Suddenly a great company of the heavenly host [literally armies] appeared with the angel**, *praising God and saying, "Glory to God in the highest heaven and on earth peace to those on whom his favor rests."* (Luke 2:8-9 NIV)

The shepherds are not gently wakened from their slumbers by rosy-cheeked cherubs with harps. They are terrified by the vision of angel warriors. This choir is a literal multitudinous heavenly army.

Their choral symphony is a victory celebration. These angels do not come to declare a truce or sign an amnesty. They herald the long-prophesied end of hostilities between heaven and hell. This is a peace born of conquest. The arrival of this bound and bundled infant signals D-day has arrived, and the groaning of all creation will soon come to an end.

Jesus' conquest over all the power of the enemy frames our understanding of spiritual warfare.

In the wilderness, Jesus resists every temptation of the devil as the second Adam—our first father having failed the test in the garden. Jesus is tempted for forty days, (just as Israel was tested for forty years in the wilderness). Our Lord had to endure the worst that Satan could throw at him: *And when the devil had ended every temptation, he departed from him* (Luke 4:13). Not until the cross, the hour and power of darkness, does Jesus face a more severe test.

Following the temptation, Jesus marches through Palestine with power. Consider the time Jesus casts out the legion of devils. Jesus and the disciples are crossing the sea to the Gerasene region. On the way, Jesus calms the stormy sea with a word of command: *Peace be still!* (Mark 4:39) Immediately following, he rebukes a legion of demons and calms a storm tossed and tormented soul. As a postscript, the man is described as *clothed and in his right mind* (Mark 5:1-20).

The cross is the decisive battle in heavens' war of conquest. Jesus' victory at the cross and resurrection is likened to the military conquests of Roman legions. The Roman general Scipio never lost a battle. He led Roman forces to defeat the elephant armies of Hannibal; the greatest enemy Rome ever faced. Returning from his conquests, Scipio led a triumphal procession, the army following, captive enemies in his train, down the heart of the city on the Appian Way, to the deafening and uproarious praise of the whole city. He shared the glory of his victory and the fruits of his conquest with the whole city.

This military metaphor applies to Jesus' victory:

You ascended on high, leading a host of captives in your train and receiving gifts. (Psalm 68:18)

He disarmed the rulers and authorities and put them to open shame, by triumphing over them in him. (Colossians 2:15)

The outcome of the war between Christ and the devil was certain, but the battle was not staged. In the suffering of his Son, the Father was wounded, his heart torn. God's suffering in the Son outweighs all the torment on all battlefields of human history.

All the fiery pains on battle fields,
On fever beds where sick men toss,
And in that human cry he yields,
To anguish on the cross.
—C.F. Alexander

The Son himself bears the fatal scars of war, enduring temptations that threatened to bend and break him. Jesus endured the full malice and hostility of sinful humanity. He was physically lashed and crucified with instruments of torment. We can never take for granted the price paid for our deliverance:

He was pierced for our transgressions; he was crushed for our iniquities ... By oppression and judgment, he was taken away; and as for his generation, who considered that he was cut off out of the land of the living, stricken for the transgression of my people? (Isaiah 53:5, 8)

In his first fall, Satan was expelled and cast down to hell by Michael and the angel armies.

There was no longer any place for [the dragon and his fallen angels] in heaven. (Revelation 12:8)

God ... did not spare the angels when they sinned but cast them into hell and committed them to chains of gloomy darkness to be kept until the judgment. (2 Peter 2:4)

Because Jesus was born, lived a holy life, died on the cross, and rose from the dead, Satan fell a second time. At the cross, Satan is cast down with eternal finality. Jesus said, *I saw Satan fall like lightning from heaven* (Luke 10:18). This is the accomplishment of Christ. The purpose for which Jesus came and died is summarized by John as the annihilation of the evil forces arrayed against heaven: The son of man came *to destroy the works of the devil* (1 John 3:8).

Satan is a vanquished foe. His power against the church is subject to God and can inflict no lasting harm. *In all these things we are more than conquerors through him who loved us... Nothing can separate us from the love of God in Christ* (Romans 8:37-39).

We fight our battles against evil in the interim between Jesus' first and second coming, between Satan's defeat at the cross and his eternal fiery destruction. For now, the dragon is permitted to harass and persecute the Church. Yet this dragon is on a leash— a leash held by Christ.

This has implications for our spiritual battles. Jesus announces: *All authority in heaven and earth has been given to me* (Matthew 28:18). The new covenant Church lives in full realization of Jesus' finished work and final conquest of Satan. We are armed with the resurrection power of Christ.

> *Behold, I have given you authority to tread on serpents and scorpions, and over all the power of the enemy, and nothing shall hurt you.* (Luke 10:19)

Spiritual warfare is warfare with a capital "S." We engage and win our battles by the Spirit of God. Jesus was driven by the Spirit to resist the devil (Mark 1:12,13). Jesus cast out demons by the Spirit of God (Matthew 12:18). Paul exhorts every Christian soldier to wield the sword of the Spirit, and to always pray in the Spirit. (Ephesians 6:12,18). Discerning the spirits is a gift of the Holy Spirit (1 Corinthians 12:10). The seven sons of Sceva pay a humiliating price for trying to do spiritual warfare apart from the Holy Spirit (Acts 19:13-17).

Prayer Power

In the war of the worlds, Christians are emissaries of heaven, exiles on earth, and enemies of hell. This "worldview" is the seedbed for powerful prayer. With eyes of faith, we look back and remember what Jesus accomplished in his first coming. In faith, we raise our eyes to heaven and direct our prayers to the glorious throne of Christ. As the Day of the Lord approaches, with eyes of faith we keep our gaze on the horizon of his imminent coming.

Divine power is given to every believer in prayer. If God's gift of power is to be internalized, actualized, and exercised, it must also be received! Power is not a given to be taken for granted. If we fail to ask, we ask to fail. Prayer is the means God gives us to receive the power of the Holy Spirit for holiness of life and effectiveness in evangelism.

Before they head into battle with the world and devils, Jesus tells the disciples to *stay in the city until you are clothed with power from on high* (Luke 24:49). The posture of waiting in none other than prayer (Acts 1:4, 8, 14). *Those who wait upon the Lord shall renew their strength* (Isaiah 40:31).

The book of Acts is a case study on the power of prayer. (see 1:14, 2:1-4, 2:42, 4:23, 31, 6:4, 7, 12:5, 10, 13:1-4). We shall treat this topic in later chapters, in the meantime, consider how Paul prays for power for the Ephesian believers, that they would *be strengthened with power through his Spirit in their inner being* (Ephesians 3:15). Paul prays that the Colossian Christians may be *strengthened with all power, according to his glorious might for all endurance and patience with joy* (Colossians 1:11).

The book of Revelation summarizes the cosmic power of our prayers to change the very tide of history. Prior to the sounding of the seven trumpets, heaven is silent and stalled. When God's people unite in supplication, our prayers are cast to earth to bring shattering changes:

> *When he opened the seventh seal, there was silence in heaven for about half an hour. And I saw the seven angels who stand before God, and seven trumpets were given to them. Another angel, who had a golden censer, came and stood at the altar. He was given much incense to offer, with the prayers of all God's people, on the golden altar in front of the throne. The smoke of the incense, together with the prayers of God's people, went up before God from the angel's hand. Then the angel took the censer, filled it with fire from the altar, and hurled it on the earth; and there came peals of thunder, rumblings, flashes of lightning and an earthquake.* (Revelation 8:1-4 NIV)

How powerful and purposeful are our prayers! Like the smoke of fragrant incense that rises to the Lord, godly prayers are mixed with the bloodied coals from the altar of Christ's sacrifice. Heaven's forces stand in abeyance until the Father approves the burning incense of prayer. When Christians offer prayer in the mediation of Christ, God Almighty shatters the enemy, destroys their strongholds, and summons the nations to account.

The Fast-Approaching Final Day Fills Out the Picture

The science of cosmology is more than the study of how the created universe works. The questions of where we are headed and how our universe meets its end are at the forefront of cosmological investigation. There have been centuries of theorizing and speculating concerning the origin and destiny of the universe. Current scientific theory is that everything started from an explosion of near infinite dimensions. The universe in all its power, splendor, and glory was flung out into the infinite void. The cosmos with its hundreds of billion galaxies is expanding until, in the unimaginably distant future, every nebula, galaxy, star, and world will burn out and die.

Christian cosmology is eschatological—that is, it is concerned with how the human story plays out. The inexorable approach of the Day of the Lord nails down the end point of our spiritual warfare. The rapidly approaching final battle sets the trajectory and determines the destiny of all human history.

The cosmic clock is ticking and will soon strike midnight! The universe will not grind to a halt. Nor will the battle between the worlds of heaven, hell, and earth rage forever. Jesus Christ and his heavenly armies will descend from heaven and *[destroy] every rule and every authority and power* (1 Corinthians 15:24).

The Day of the Lord is the day of the final conflagration. The hordes of Satan and all his earthly allies will gather against the Lord and his Christ. This will signal the end of our history.

> *And they assembled them at the place that in Hebrew is called Armageddon.* (Revelation 16:16)

> *I saw heaven opened, and behold, a white horse! The one sitting on it is called Faithful and True, and in righteousness he judges and makes war. His eyes are like a flame of fire, and on his head are many diadems … Then I saw the beast and the kings of the earth and their armies gathered together to wage war against the rider on the horse and his army.* (Revelation 11-12, 19)

The outcome is utter devastation of all those gathered against Christ:

And the beast was captured, and with it the false prophet who had performed the signs on its behalf ... The two of them were thrown alive into the fiery lake of burning sulphur... The devil was thrown into the lake of fire ... Then Death and Hades were thrown into the lake of fire... and if anyone's name was not written in the book of Life he was thrown into the lake of fire. (Revelation 19:20-21:20, 14, 15)

Yet, until the final Day of the Lord, amnesty is offered to everyone:

Seek the LORD, all you humble of the land, you who do what he commands. Seek righteousness, seek humility; perhaps you will be sheltered on the day of the LORD's anger. (Zephaniah 2:3)

The Spirit and the bride say, "Come." Let him who hears say, "Come." And let the one who is thirsty come; let the one who desires take the water of life without price. (Revelation 22:17)

Believers stand poised between the first and second coming of Jesus Christ. On one hand, we look back and fill our souls with the joyous realization of all that Christ's death and resurrection means to our warfare. "It is finished!" echoes through the ages. On the other hand, in the interim, we follow Christ and eagerly await his second coming. This two-fold dynamic fuels our prayers with power and informs our gospel witness with urgency.

HOW TO PRAY

A Prayer for Eyes to Be Opened

Lord Jesus, in this day of deepening darkness, an innumerable seen and unseen host gathers and surrounds your people. It is as if the prophecy has come to pass—the pit has been opened and foul spirits have been released to wreak carnage and bring confusion to the entire world. Because we bear your name, we and our children are taking the brunt of this assault. You warned us, "If they hated me, they will also hate you."

We confess we often feel overwhelmed and even helpless against this hostile conspiracy. As we pray, we fix our eyes on you this day. Because you were born and dwelt among us, we are your body. Because you died on the cross, we share in your triumph over evil. Because you were raised in power, we too are raised in resurrection power. As we await the final conquest, we know that we are more than conquerors in your victory. Therefore, we will not despair. We will not flee. We will take our stand and stand firm. Lord, fill the heart of our prayers with this realization. Grant us to know your presence and be filled with your power that we might discern and engage the enemy, putting to death the deeds of the flesh, resisting the devil, and boldly proclaiming your victory to those in captivity. Amen.

TESTIMONY

Kneeling in Prayer, Standing in Courage
From a School Board Trustee in Canada

Amy taught school for several years and became alarmed when trustees supported and promoted SOGI programs (Sexual Orientation and Gender Identity) and endorsed practicing native rituals for elementary-age children. She shared this testimony:

> "Several years ago, I ran in a local election to become a school trustee. Though technically qualified to hold this position in school governance (as a certified teacher myself with adequate knowledge of the school system, two young children, and meeting all the legal requirements to hold office), I felt incredibly intimidated. I am not what most people would picture when they hear the term "politician." Nonetheless, it was a clear call from the Lord to step up, and after a difficult campaign, I was elected.
>
> Now, at the beginning of my second term, I can confidently say I fully understand the position, its authority as well as its limitations. For my first four years on the school board, I was the recipient of bullying, ridicule, and general mistreatment. The intensity of these blows felt doubly real to me because I was also receiving similar treatment in my private life at the time. Although from an outsider's perspective, this would have looked like personal attacks, I knew it to be part of a much larger, spiritual battle. My response was to be on my knees in prayer with fellow believers (fighting in the spiritual realm) and on my feet standing for what is right and true (holding ground on the battlefield here on earth).
>
> The enemy would like nothing more than for the upcoming generations to be deceived and destroyed, and the education system (and nuclear family) is one of his current playing fields to accomplish those ends. Being in this arena has opened my eyes to the scope of dangerous and deceptive ideas that our children are exposed to these days.

At the same time as children are encouraged to participate in spiritual practices, they are reminded of the "narrow-mindedness" and "bigotry" of the Christian faith. Students are celebrated for identifying as another gender and reprimanded for sharing beliefs in gender assigned by God.

Yet even in this disheartening climate, I have been encouraged. Concerted prayer has led to exciting changes this year. An additional Christian was voted onto the board after the last election, and a respectful chairperson replaced the toxic one, leading to a healthier environment and bringing relief to many employees. Parents and community members are becoming more engaged in decision making, and inflammatory media reporting seems to have subsided for the moment.

God has taught me about his faithfulness and trustworthiness, how to turn the other cheek, the necessity of relying on him, the power of praying according to his will, and the blessings of being supported by a family of believers. God's presence carries me through a very real and deeply dark valley.
His Word is my authority, and His love gives me the courage I need to persevere each day."

CHAPTER 2

Discern the Times, Tell the Times

"Time is the wisest counselor of all."

—Pericles

"Ring them bells for the blind and the deaf,
Ring them bells for all of us who are left,
Ring them bells for the chosen few,
Who will judge the many when the game is through.
Ring them bells for the time that flies,
For the child that cries
When the innocence dies"

—Bob Dylan, *Ring Them Bells*

We concluded Chapter 1 by explaining the temporal dimension of a Christian cosmology. The trajectory and destiny of our world can only be understood in reference to the second coming of Christ to restore all things. In chapter 2 we continue this thread by adding this application; to wage spiritual warfare effectively we need to discern the time we live in and tell the time to the world around us.

Knowing the times is an urgent priority. Ignorance of the times signals an ignorance of the present purposes of God. *There is no longer a prophet among us who knows how long* (Psalm 74:9). In 1 Chronicles, we read an important clause that highlights the vital role of those who discern the day and hour: *Of Issachar,* ***men who had understanding of the times****, to know what Israel ought to do…* (12:32). Without men and women who discern the times, the Church wanders about in uncertainty, and the world remains heedless to coming judgment.

We have found that believers under persecution are aware of the present conflict of kingdoms. They view the world through a supernatural lens. They discern the present work of God and activity of Satan. They have a heightened awareness of what we might call "Kingdom time."

In North America, for the most part, many Christians seem unaware of the supernatural dimension of current events. We fail to "tell the time." We have fallen asleep to the present danger of the enemy as well as the surpassing power of our Lord.

God's People Can Know the Times

We might no longer require the office of prophet or seer, but prophetic insight into the times is as essential now as it was in Old Testament times, as Paul makes this clear:

> *Besides this you know the time, that the hour has come for you to wake from sleep … The night is far gone; the day is at hand.* (Romans 13:11-12)

God gives prophetic insight to the wise and discerning so they can understand the tide of current events, discern the powers that orchestrate them, and announce the time to the Church and world.

Jesus uses the metaphor of the fig tree when he exhorts his followers to know the signs of the times:

> ***Now when these [end times] begin to take place, straighten up and raise your heads, because your redemption is drawing near.*** *And he told them a parable: "Look at the fig tree, and any other tree. As soon as they come out in leaf you see for yourselves and know that summer is already near. So also, when you see these things taking place, you know that the kingdom of God is near."* (Luke 21:28-31)

A believer can know what Jesus is doing at the present time. *No longer do I call you servants, for the servant does not know what his master is doing* (John 15:15). As we study the world through the lens of Scripture and in prayer, and in Christian community, we discern the time of day. Jesus has given us the Holy Spirit so we will know where we are in cosmic history: *He will declare to you the things that are to come* (John 16:13). The Spirit enlightens us as we study and apply Scripture to our present day. This promise to know the times is continually refreshed in every new generation.

Paul also affirms that believers can know the times: *Now concerning the times and the seasons, brothers, you have no need to have anything written to you* (1 Thessalonians 5:1). Those whom God gives wisdom will know the time; those who are ignorant will not.

In contrast, Jesus criticizes his opponents because they don't know the times:

You hypocrites, you know how to interpret the appearances of the earth and sky, but why do you not know how to interpret the present time? (Luke 12:56)

The Pharisees, scribes, and lawyers were unable to tell the time. Though they "played by the book," they missed the greatest sign of their time, indeed of all time, the arrival of the Messiah in the fullness of time. Consider that the Sanhedrin preached from the Scriptures every Sabbath, yet because they failed to discern their times in relation to Christ or warn the people, their messages proved useless. Unbelief makes one blind to the times.

We Tell Time for the World

It is not enough to know the time: we must also tell the time. When I was a teenager in the late sixties, our "counterculture" kept time by a Doomsday Clock. The clock represented human history on a 24-hour watch face. Midnight signaled the annihilation of mankind. As the clock ticked precariously close to midnight, we measured the hours and seconds by the Iron Curtain and the threat of nuclear war, the Vietnam conflict, and the pollution and destruction of the environment. Apocalyptic markers today might include the Israeli-Palestinian conflicts, threats of pandemics, and global warming. Meant to encourage urgency and purpose, this ticking down of time creates fear and anxiety.

There is growing awareness among believers today that the Day of the Lord is not far off. At prayer workshops, I often ask; "If all human history is a 24-hour clock, what is the time of day? In your best judgment, is it morning, afternoon, evening, or night?" The response I hear most often is night. Probing deeper, I ask, "Is it dusk, or nearing midnight?" Younger Christians tend to vote for dusk. Older Christians estimate near midnight.

The Bible contains a cosmological clock that tells "Kingdom time." From Genesis to Revelation, the Scriptures count down time in relation to Christ's return. Believers ask, "What time is it in relation to the second coming?" Midnight for the Christian represents the final Day of the Lord. The prophets warned, *the great day of the Lord is near, near and hastening fast* (Zephaniah 1:14).

In several Kingdom parables, Jesus exhorts believers to be ready, to have their lamps filled and trimmed, to stay awake, to keep their eyes on the horizon because his return is imminent and will come at an hour that we least expect. The day nears when the weeds will be separated from the wheat, the goats from the sheep, and the bad fish from the good. Wheat, sheep, and good fish will be harvested for eternal joy. Weeds, goats, and bad fish will be cast into darkness and unquenchable fire. Keeping an eye on the time, every day of the Christian life should be filled with expectancy and urgency of purpose. We are responsible to tell time to the world. When the Church warns of coming judgment, she is like Big Ben in midst of cities and nations, letting citizens know where the world stands as it approaches a fixed time of reckoning for every word, thought, and deed.

Recent fires in Hawaii devastated an entire island because the warning systems were in disrepair. When believers preach to an unbeliever about Christ imminent return to judge the world, they are like an early warning system for natural disasters like fires, tornadoes, hurricanes, or tsunamis. We sound the siren that signals a coming air raid. If we are silent and fail to sound the alarm, the devastation will be complete.

Where there is no prophetic vision, the people cast off restraint (Proverbs 29:18). In contrast, heralding the coming judgment slows the process of godlessness and lawlessness. When the world heeds the warning, the fear of God restrains the relentless advance of sin.

Gospel proclamation includes a warning of judgment (either convicting or condemning the hearer) and a declaration of victory over Satan. We see this confirmed in the words of Jesus concerning the work of the Holy Spirit:

And when he comes, [the Spirit] will convict the world concerning sin and righteousness and judgment ... concerning judgment, because the ruler of this world is judged. (John 16:8, 11)

Evangelism, in one sense, is telling the time to the world. Consider how Paul preaches to the Athenians. After pointing out the folly of their idolatry, he ends his sermon with a warning.

The times of ignorance God overlooked, but now he commands all people everywhere to repent, because he has fixed a day on which he will judge the world in righteousness by a man he has appointed; and of this he has given assurance to all by raising him from the dead. (Acts 17:30-31)

Paul also preaches about a final day when sharing the gospel with the governor Felix: ... *he reasoned about righteousness and self-control and the coming judgment* (Acts 24:25).

When we tell the time of day, we are preaching a powerful and relevant message of repentance and hope for our day. If we fail to warn of coming judgment our messages will fail to move hearers to repentance. If we fail to sound the alarm, we will be held responsible (Ezekiel 3:18,19).

Signs of the Times

Storm clouds are gathering in the West and around the world. Since the coming of Christ, both good and evil have been ripening; good like figs on a fig tree and evil like weeds in an untended field. As history proceeds discerning believers mature in understanding of good and evil.

> *Solid food is for the mature, for those who have their powers of discernment trained by constant practice to distinguish good from evil.* (Hebrews 5:14)

After millennia of warfare, we are now aware that unseen opponents to the gospel are sharpening their focus and intensifying their attack on Christ and his people.

Believers today have lost their urgency because they have lost their sense of the imminence of Christ's return. When someone preaches that the Day of the Lord is soon arriving, the common response is, "Sure, but Christians have always thought the end of the world is near." That is true. Relative to eternal life or eternal judgment, the end of the world is minutes away. In every era, Christ is at the door. However, history is not static. As the last days approach, apocalyptic signs multiply and intensify, hastening the end.

To illustrate, I recall a missionary from Africa explaining the repeated sequence of gathering clouds and eventual storms that signal the end of the dry season in the African Savannah.

He pointed out, when the rains cease, the land dries up and becomes a dusty wasteland. Beast and land thirst and long for the rains to arrive to bring life, hope, and renewal. The earliest sign of coming rain is a few clouds gathering on a distant horizon. However, they recede. Days later, darker, and larger clouds gather, approaching even nearer. Once again, they recede. This may happen several times. At long last, billowing black clouds, thundering and pregnant, darken the entire sky and bring lightning and rain. A month-long deluge drenches the parched earth.

When dark clouds of persecution, tyranny, wars, natural disasters, famines, and plagues multiply, expectant believers lift their eyes to the horizon and wonder, "Could this be the end?" However, this is just the beginning of the birth pangs. Time and again, the signs approach and recede, and life goes on. As years go by, anti-Christian tyrants and false prophets multiply, along with times of intense persecution. Christians lift their eyes with renewed expectancy. But then another pause, perhaps a revival, and the dark clouds recede. However, near the end there is no room for doubt—blackened clouds arrive, and a deluge descends.

As the final storm draws near, the signs of the end multiply and topple over one another with chaotic violence—wars, natural disasters, tyrants, persecutions, ungodly decrees, heartless evildoers, civil wars, and the like. Godlessness and lawlessness take over. At long last, the great tribulation is here. It becomes obvious to all but the blind and heedless that the seals have been opened (Revelation 6), the trumpets are sounding (Revelation 8), and the bowls are being poured out (Revelation 16).

As the present post-resurrection age proceeds, the world speeds to its determined destiny. The gun has been loaded, the trigger cocked, and the bullet has been fired. Judgment is on its way. Lawless men and ungodly rulers are becoming more antichrist and anti-Christian. Allied to unseen evil, a rebellious humankind gathers forces, unites, and conspires, saying, *Let us burst their bonds apart and cast away their cords from us* (Psalm 2:3). Jesus prophesied these signs so we might be prepared for his coming. Unbelievers will be caught unawares and will stand naked and ashamed before the throne of judgment:

> *Now concerning the times and seasons, brothers, you have no need to have anything written to you. For you yourselves are fully aware that the day of the Lord will come like a thief in the night. While people are saying, "there is peace and security," then sudden destruction will come upon them as labor pains come upon a pregnant woman, and they will not escape. But you are not in the darkness, brothers, for that day to surprise you like a thief.* (1 Thessalonians 5:1-4)

As the time of the end nears, the world will shut its ears. Consider other apocalyptic events that prefigure the end of the world.

- Noah heralded the good news for 100 years until the day God closed the doors of the ark. No one heeded his message. The day of grace had ended (see 2 Peter 2:5).

- In longsuffering, God postponed judgment on the Canaanites for four generations, *until the iniquity of the Amorites is … complete* (Genesis 15:16).

- Sodom and Gomorrah were given the opportunity to repent, but loved unrighteousness and oppressed the poor, so God rained down fiery sulfur to cleanse the world of their contaminating influence (Ezekiel 16:49 and Jude 1:7).
- At the end of Israel's monarchy, God sent his prophets time and again, but they went unheeded. Time came when *there was no remedy* (2 Chronicles 36:16).
- Jesus tells us that darkness will one day descend on humankind. *Night is coming when no one can work* (John 9:4).

Alert believers live a life of patient but eager expectation for the second coming of Christ. It is time to prepare. It is time to proclaim that the Day is near and coming quickly.

Prayer: The Forefront of Spiritual Warfare

A strong life of prayer is the substratum for knowing the times. As we contemplate the word and study the world in prayer, the revelations of Scripture come to life and present relevance. Consider Daniel. His prayer life yields discernment both for the present and the future. Following a colossal prayer of repentance, the angel comes to Daniel with surpassing revelations about the future of the world:

> *While I was speaking in prayer, the man Gabriel …*
> *came to me in swift flight at the time of the evening sacrifice. …*
> *"O Daniel, I have come out to give you insight and understanding.*
> *At the beginning of your pleas for mercy a word went out …"*
> (Daniel 9:21-23)

Those who are strong in prayer will gain insight into the present future workings and of our Lord.

HOW TO PRAY

A Prayer to Know the Times and Tell the Time

Heavenly Father, we thank you that we are not suspended in mid-air, somewhere between your Son's first and second coming. As friends of your Son, we are gifted with a present awareness of your work in the world. As you reveal the times, we are invited into partnership with your working in the world. We see that you restrain and guide the very nations of the world; carry out your marvelous saving purposes; and overcome all the forces of evil arrayed against you and your people. Fill us with hope and courage as we see the rising light of your coming day. Grant that we heed your promise and command to make disciples of all nations with the same hope and urgency of the first disciples.

Give us the words and the boldness to tell unbelievers the time of day—to warn our neighbors of the coming day of reckoning and retribution and grant our words to have saving effect. As the nations gather to oppose your truth by decree and by coercion, we echo the prayer of the apostle and give you full- hearted thanks that we have been delivered from the domain of darkness and transferred to the kingdom of your beloved Son. With inner hope and Holy Spirit confidence, we ask you to grant by your mighty power that we may persevere in thankfulness; help us to *live a life worthy of you in every way, pleasing to you and bearing fruit in every good work; and increasing in the knowledge of God* (Colossians 1:9-13).

We pray this in Jesus' name. Amen.

TESTIMONY

From Stoned to Sober Before the Judgment Seat
My Story of Conversion

I trace my own conversion to the moment I woke up to the time of day.

I had always been hungry for drama, but not the staged variety. The pyrotechnics and wall of sound at a rock concert left me flat. I was looking for awe. At the age of 17, I was about to encounter it.

One late night I was hanging out a friend's house. We'd been smokin' and tokin'—but I wasn't feeling the sensational high I used to. I was pretty much played out when it came to getting stoned.

My friend Robbie was one of the few philosophical types I knew. After listening to troubadours like Simon and Garfunkel, he chose that evening to share some apocalyptic insights. As he read excerpts from *Memories Dreams and Reflections* by French priest Teilhard de Chardin, I nodded with dull incomprehension.

Then Robbie pulled out another book. This time, it was the big one—a Bible. He looked me in the eye and said, "Let me read something to you. It's really far out. My grandmother read it to me the other day." Robbie's grandma was a hard-core tongues-and-miracles Pentecostal. She trod the path of life with determined steps and grim visage. For her, each day was next to last. She was kind of scary.

Robbie read from Matthew 24, sharing Jesus' warnings about the coming apocalypse. As he read the chapter, Jesus' words piled up, gaining weight and momentum, one cosmic warning after another.

> *Many false Christs will arise. Do not follow them* (24:5).
> *There will be wars and rumors of war …* (24:6).
> *Because of lawlessness, men's love will grow cold …* (24:12).
> *One will be taken and one will be left …* (24:40).

These words hit me like a two by four in the head. I was shocked into sobriety. The warnings ran through my mind with 220-volt force, penetrating to my core. My day of reckoning had come. I heard a guilty verdict. I was powerless to defend myself. As the words echoed, I entered a timeless zone. The music played on, but I only heard the foreboding words.

There will be wars and rumors of war. It was the late 60s. Vietnam, the Cold War, and the atom bomb are present threats.

Many false Christs will arise. At the time, Eastern gurus, divine incarnations, and Christian cult leaders were springing up every other week. The previous year, Jim Jones, founder of the Peoples Temple, had led 909 people in a suicide of biblical proportions.

Men's love will grow cold. No imagination needed here. The Velcro of relationships had worn thin. Friendship was scarce and loneliness reigned.

One will be taken, and another will be left. This was a new concept for me, but the meaning was clear: I was one of those who would be left behind.

Then the final declaration hit me with brass knuckle's simplicity: Like the lightning which shines from the east to the west … *so will be the coming of the Son of Man* (24:27).

Imagine a thunderstorm in the dead of night, 200 million volts of lightning cracking and careening across a black sky. In blinding light, shadows dissolve. Only the real remains. I didn't just hear words; I was having a vision.

The New Testament word for vision is *orasis*. It signifies an immediate experience of divine reality. The visible disappears. Like a blinding camera flash, the words leave an after-image as the light bursts on the inner retina of my soul. Decades later, I can still close my eyes and recall everything in color and detail. The picture is inscribed on the inside of my heart and mind.

While I sat fixed to my chair, somewhere between trance and shock, Robbie was utterly unaware of what was going on inside me. High and dry, he finished reading and looked at me.

On the one hand, I was terrified. On the other hand, I was feeling the awe I'd waited a lifetime for. It captured my every cell. I realized; "God is speaking to me … in this room … right now!"

Hammer to anvil, Jesus' words broke open my soul. It was my 'big bang' as everything exploded out of nothing. *In the beginning was the Word* (John 1:1). Detonated, these words can't be capped. As Annie Dillard writes, "We are mixing up a batch of TNT. We should all wear crash helmets."

There was a warning within this vision: "John, you're in trouble." I knew beyond doubt that I was on the other side, the wrong side of the coming Kingdom Jesus is talking about.

I realized I had debts—massive reparations. If I didn't heed this warning, there would be hell to pay. *Enter the rocks and hide in the dust before the terror of the Lord, and the splendor of his majesty* (Isaiah 2:10).

At the same time, somewhere in the middle of this maelstrom, another realization emerged. Out of the chaos, I heard another voice (I wasn't sure if it was my wakened self or God); "If there's a day of judgment; there is also a day of pardon."

The threat brought a promise. If there's a final day, there must also be a tomorrow on the other side—the day after the final day. If there's an end to the world, then there is a beginning beyond it. Minutes after I was wakened by the alarm, I felt beckoned. God had come at me from both sides. God warns and he invites, he frowns, and he smiles.

I recognized this voice. It wasn't a stranger talking to me. He'd always been talking to me. It was an outer voice speaking deep within. The warnings and invitations had always been there. But now, they were so deafening I couldn't fail to hear them.

CHAPTER 3

Eyes Open to the Unholy Alliance

> "My prayer is that when I die, all of hell will rejoice that I am out of the fight."
>
> —C.S. Lewis

As we are learning, in our warfare it is critical that we understand the times—especially the present times in relation to the end times. A serious and sober study of eschatology, literally "a knowledge of the last things," is essential in engaging evil on all fronts—cosmic, cultural, within the Church, and as individuals. As human history marches to its appointed terminus, the strategic and concerted assaults of Satan and his allies intensify.

In the Bible, we are warned that in the last days when the fifth trumpet sounds, a key will open *the shaft of the bottomless pit.* Demonic spirits will rise to the surface to be loosed upon the world (Revelation 9:1-12). This is the prelude to the judgments of the sixth and seventh trumpet, when the united seen and unseen forces of evil will gather against Christ and his people. As history advances, a malevolent union of evil forces will ripen to fruition. Finally, at the time God determines, this alliance will be birthed in its hideous fullness.

Our present times are tense with apocalyptic expectation. As evil invades and infiltrates our world, even unbelievers sense that the times are growing darker. This should not surprise us. In several places, the Bible reveals that the closer we get to the end, wickedness will intensify:

But mark this: There will be terrible times in the last days. People will be lovers of themselves, lovers of money, boastful, proud, abusive, disobedient to their parents, ungrateful, unholy, without love, unforgiving, slanderous, without self-control, brutal, not lovers of the good, treacherous, rash, conceited, lovers of pleasure rather than lovers of God—having a form of godliness but denying its power. Have nothing to do with such people. (2 Timothy 3:1-5 NIV)

In a final gasp, this manifestation of evil will have an expressly demonic character. Paul exhorts the early Christians to pay attention to the signs of lawlessness in their day. He warns them to be prepared for the hour when demonic forces will be fully manifest:

The coming of the lawless one will be in accordance with how Satan works. He will use all sorts of displays of power through signs and wonders that serve the lie, and all the ways that wickedness deceives those who are perishing … so that all will be condemned who have not believed the truth but have delighted in wickedness. (2 Thessalonians 2:9-12 NIV)

The apostle John instructs Christians to be on guard. After the cross, an antichrist influence entered the world; this influence will continue to increase as the final day draws near:

Children, it is the last hour, and as you have heard that the antichrist is coming, so now many antichrists have come. Therefore we know it is the last hour. (1 John 2:18)

The Armageddon Alliance[5]

The book of Revelation graphically depicts the acceleration of evil the Church will face in the end times. John paints the canvas of history with future expectations that are filled with present relevance. Studying Chapters 12 through 18, we learn that as the final day approaches, seen and unseen evil powers will amalgamate:

The sixth angel poured out his bowl ... Then I saw three impure spirits that looked like frogs; they came out of the mouth of the dragon, out of the mouth of the beast and out of the mouth of the false prophet. They are demonic spirits that perform signs, and they go out to the kings of the whole world, to gather them for the battle on the great day of God Almighty.

"Look, I come like a thief! Blessed is the one who stays awake and remains clothed, so as not to go naked and be shamefully exposed." Then they gathered the kings together to the place that in Hebrew is called Armageddon. The seventh angel poured out his bowl into the air, and out of the temple came a loud voice from the throne, saying, "It is done!" (Revelation 16:12-17 NIV)

As the world nears its terminus, there will be a "surfacing" and uniting of demonic powers that will overwhelm humankind, namely the dragon, the beasts of land and sea, and Babylon. False prophets, world rulers, and many peoples will give their allegiance to these demonic powers. This unholy alliance of seen and unseen powers will rise to ravage the earth and make war with Christ and his Church.

Do not let these monsters of evil terrify you. Rest assured that these creatures of darkness are on the short leash of the sovereign rule of Jesus Christ:

They have conquered [the dragon] by the by the blood of the Lamb and the word of their testimony. (Revelation 12:11)

[Christ] disarmed the rulers and authorities and put them to open shame, by triumphing over them in him. (Colossians 2:15)

---

[5] I have relied on *The Triumph of the Lamb: A Commentary on Revelation* by Dennis Johnson, to confirm my insights and understandings on the following analysis.

Isaac Watts, in a rousing hymn, "We're Marching through Immanuel's Land," gives this encouragement to Christians: 'Then let our songs abound, and every tear be dry. We're marching through Immanuel's land to greater lands on high." When facing evil face to face, readiness, not fear, is our posture.

The Architects of Evil

The dragon, Satan, the Devil, is the main deceiver and adversary behind the fall of our first parents, the crucifixion of Christ, and the final battle against the Lord and his Church.

Until the end of this age, Satan remains the Church's most resolute enemy. Though crippled by the cross, his power is great and will be increasingly manifest as history proceeds.

Satan is called a murderer, the accuser of the brethren, the father of lies, and a deceiving angel of light. Cast down from heaven to hell, his rebellion drew one-third of the heavenly angelic host to hell. These fallen angels are now the demons and armies of wickedness under his command. Carrying out Satan's schemes, they propagate idolatry and inflict blindness on the entire world:

The god of this world has blinded the minds of the unbelievers, to keep them from seeing the light of the gospel of the glory of Christ, who is the image of God. (2 Corinthians 4:4)

The dragon's grand strategy is to form a hostile allegiance between the powers of this world, the beast of violence, the false prophets of lies, and a worldly and willing Babylon. The dragon's last stand will be when he marshals all these antichrist forces for the battle at Armageddon.

The beast that rises from the sea represents ungodly and coercive political power. The power of the beast is exercised to subjugate the peoples and nations of the world and to persecute the Church. Every government is appointed by God to institute laws that encourage the obedient and punish the lawbreaker. When rulers abandon the fear of God, they attempt to "take over for God." They inevitably fail to execute justice for their people or protect the mission of the church (1 Timothy 2:1-4). This opens the door to a plague of antichrist wickedness.

The beast rising from the land has horns like a lamb. This beast fills the present age with lies and propaganda in support of the beast of power. Some identify this diabolic monstrosity with the antichrist and the man of lawlessness.

In the world arena, this beast is behind those dictators and tyrants who commandeer the media under their domain, filling the news and airwaves with crafty deceptions and lies.

This beast has "horns like a lamb" and leads the world to worship the beast of power. The guise of a lamb is to hide underlying devilish intent.

Babylon is the world city, a promiscuous seductress whose allurements and base indulgences infect the entire world. Unlike temple prostitutes of that day—many of whom were slaves, orphans, or foundlings trafficked into prostitution—this adulteress plies her trade for the sheer pleasure of seducing and making victims of the innocent. Her kind of lechery is described in Ezekiel:

Men give gifts to all prostitutes, but you gave your gifts to all your lovers, bribing them to come to you from every side with your whorings. So you were different from other women in your whorings. No one solicited you to play the whore, and you gave payment, while no payment was given to you; therefore you were different. (Ezekiel 16:33-34)

Babylon is the *great city that has dominion over the king of the earth* (Revelation 17:18) "City" in this case means more than a geopolitical entity; it is an amalgam of human intent, characterized by unrepentant and accelerating corruption. Babylon rides on all the waters of the earth, transcending any city but infecting them all.

Recalling the Tower of Babel, our world has become an interconnected world city rife with the influence of Babylon. An unrestrained, idolatrous, image-laden world guzzles down her intoxicating cup, becoming drunk with sexual temptation, acquisitiveness, and immorality. Fueled by ceaseless media blandishments, through powerful engines of envy and greed, today's Babylon tears down every religious and ideological barrier. She tempts us all saying, "You can keep your religion. Just enjoy what I offer!"

Consider the degeneration, oppression, and sexual immorality endemic to the ancient cities of Sodom, Nineveh, Babylon, Tyre, Sidon, and Rome. Behind a shiny exterior, Vancouver, Toronto, New York, Los Angeles, London, Dubai, and other world cities are likewise drunk with the Babylon forces of seduction.

We might compare Babylon to the ingenious insect called the antlion. This stealth predator digs a pit in sandy soil to capture its prey. Once a victim enters, the antlion throws sand at its victims, so the insect falls down the slope, sliding inexorably into waiting jaws. In the spirit of Babylon, voracious and predatory advertising lures the unsuspecting, multiplying images and videos of carefree, no-consequence lust and luxury until victims are devoured by their own indulgence.

In our day it is impossible to avoid the brazen lure of Babylon. Recently we were catching a plane in the international terminal in Lisbon, Portugal. To get to the gate we had to pass through an acre wide duty-free shop. It was a panoply of lust and luxury, accompanied by tempting images advertising carefree youthful sexuality; shiny, timeless celebrity promotions; the latest in brand name blandishments—all crying out for veneration and purchase. What is true of the Lisbon international terminal is true of most other airports of the world.

Once you get on the plane and you are forced to watch a series of promotions, especially offering thousands of travel points to sign up for credit cards. Before you watch a movie, you are required to watch three or four ads about the latest cars and other accoutrements for the prosperous.

Distracting from the painful realities of aging, along with inevitable decline and death, endless vacations for our "twilight years" has replaced heaven as the hope for the elderly. Retire at 55 and ride off into the sunset of endless beaches, waterfront cafés, trendy galleries, escorted Safaris—all in the best resorts and hotels the world has to offer.

Babylon, the world city, or Cosmopolis, markets the world to the world. Babylon tempts everyone but targets the worldly wealthy. *The love of many will grow cold* (Matthew 24:12).

Increasingly, the poor are left behind. This chart illustrates the increasing disparity between rich and poor:

Share of Global Income Over Time[6]

Year	Richest 20%	Poorest 20%	Ratio of poor to rich
1960	70.2	2.3	30:1
1970	73.9	2.3	32:1
1980	76.3	1.7	45:1
1989	82.7	1.4	59:1
1997	90.0	1.0	74:1

Whole nations and an entire generation are infected with the avaricious spirit of Babylon. At the heart of the global vanity fair lies a vacuous promise that the good life is ceaseless stimulation, immersive entertainment, digital engagement, all designed to satisfy the craving of a digitalized, commercialized, and sexualized world. This is a worldly cocktail packaged in sensuous images, offering unhindered accessibility to a world of leisure, lust, and luxury.

> *Babylon was a golden cup in the LORD's hand, making all the earth drunken; the nations drank of her wine; therefore the nations went mad.* (Jeremiah 51:7)

Babylon will drink a different cup in her time and day. And that is why God tells us to come out from among her.

> *The great city was split into three parts, and the cities of the nations fell, and God remembered Babylon the great, to make her drain the cup of the wine of the fury of his wrath.* (Revelation 16:19)

There can be no truce or alliance with this Babylon spirit. Only those who renounce and refuse to comply will escape the power of her seduction:

> *Come out of her, my people, lest you take part in her sins, lest you share in her plagues; for her sins are heaped high as heaven, and God has remembered her iniquities.* (Revelation 18:4-5)

---

6 W. Ellwood, *The No Nonsense Guide to Globalization* (London: Verso, 2001), 101. For updated statistics see Peter S. Goodman, *Davos Man: How Billionaires Devoured the World* (New York: HarperCollins, 2025).

The Antichrist is described most extensively in the teaching of the apostle John. In Revelations he portrays the entire panoply of evil. In his three letters, John focuses on the antichrist. The antichrist embodies a concentration of all demonic forces. He is an enemy whose main task is to oppose and deny that Jesus Christ is God.

For many deceivers have gone out into the world, those who do not confess the coming of Jesus Christ in the flesh. Such a one is the deceiver and the antichrist. (2 John 1:7)

The antichrist is an alliance of evil spirits and false prophets:

Many false prophets have gone out into the world … every spirit that does not confess Jesus is not from God. This is the spirit of the antichrist, which you heard was coming and now is in the world already. (1 John 4:1-3)

This adversary has plagued the Church throughout history. The appearing of the antichrist is not just one event or one person appearing in future history, but the rising of a multitude of false teachers ultimately culminating in a person or time of unprecedented opposition to the gospel.

Children, it is the last hour, and as you have heard that antichrist is coming, so now many antichrists have come. Therefore, we know that it is the last hour. (1 John 2:18)

The End of the Unholy Alliance

Armageddon is where the unholy alliance will meet its doom. Scripture presages the union of world forces against Christ and the church. *Why do the nations conspire … The kings of the earth rise up and the rulers band together against the Lord and against his anointed* (Psalm 2:1-2). A descriptive portrayal of the final Armageddon is found in Ezekiel 38–39. We draw upon the series of prophecies of the final Satanic deception and gathering of the nations found in Revelation (see 13:14; 16:13-16; 17:12-14; 19:17-21; 20:7-10).

Wickedness reaches an Armageddon state when Satanic powers, false prophets, world rulers, and the apostate church gathers in concert against our Lord:

> *They assembled at the place that in Hebrew is called Armageddon…*
> *These are of one mind, and they hand over their power and authority*
> *to the beast. They will make war on the Lamb and the Lamb will*
> *conquer them.* (Revelation 16:16, 17:13-14)

In every godless age, an evil craft and power coordinates ever-broadening propaganda, a global "newspeak" of the day. In every place where God is dishonored, and the gospel opposed, unseen powers direct the plans and purposes of rulers and authorities. Underlying schemes and proven ancient strategies are orchestrated by the powers beneath the powers that be.

This ascendency of evil is not an accident; rather it is the judgment of God on a rebellious world. Steadily advancing and filling the earth, seen and unseen forces become entrenched in ruling structures so that nothing short of a mighty revival or the final coming of our Lord can destroy their strongholds. From the day of Jesus' ascension until now, this unholy alliance has been marshaling forces against his church. The first believers recognized this alliance of religious and political powers:

> *You spoke by the Holy Spirit through the mouth of your servant,*
> *our father David: "Why do the nations rage and the peoples plot*
> *in vain? The kings of the earth rise up and the rulers band together*
> *against the Lord and against his anointed one." Indeed, Herod and*
> *Pontius Pilate met together with the Gentiles and the people of*
> *Israel in this city to conspire against your holy servant Jesus,*
> *whom you anointed. They did what your power and will had*
> *decided beforehand should happen.* (Acts 4:25-28)

The astonishing speed of the ascendency and anti-life, anti-God policies and practices in our time indicates a coalition of seen and unseen powers. Consider the current assaults on human dignity couched in language and individual freedom. Recalling Molech, the god who devours children through human sacrifice, tens of millions of unborn children are offered up each year as an offering to "reproductive rights." With increasing force and scope, governments champion and implement a "right to die" policy for the aged, infirm, and handicapped. An all-out assault on our Creator's design is evident in the rapid mobilization of legislators, scientists, medical professionals, lawyers, and leaders who promote gender alteration as a human right, often regardless of age or decision-making abilities. As the prophet laments of his nation, *You devour people, and you bereave your nation of children* (Ezekiel 36:13).

Facilitating this amalgam of evil is the accelerated formation of a single global consciousness through the various forms of communication technology. It is not fear mongering to hear echoes of the Tower of Babel when the united human enterprise becomes an all-out defiance of heaven's sovereign rule: *Let us build ourselves a city and a tower … lest we be dispersed over the face of the whole earth* (Genesis 11:4).

This shared global consciousness is profoundly spiritual. New gods have ascended to the top of the pantheon. In previous ages, when threatened by natural disasters, people everywhere would "call on their gods" to deliver them. Usurping the Creator, today's architects of global consciousness fuel a fear of extinction. Human ingenuity, science, and technology have become the go-to gods to solve this paralyzing anxiety. Those who attempt to save the world without acknowledging God are the architects of evil representing the one *who opposes and exalts himself above every so called god or object of worship… proclaiming himself to be God* (2 Thessalonians 2:4).

Appeals to reason and common decency seem to be of little avail in slowing the advance of wickedness. Casual Christianity is helpless to withstand the swift and deepening tide of evil.

How to Discern, Engage, and Conquer

Godless alliances bring us closer to the final conflict. Cities, nations, and rulers are coalescing to oppose Christianity. More than half the world, 60 countries at present count, is conscious and deliberate in its antichrist aims. Communism remains overtly against Christ. Militant Islam targets Christianity as a chief enemy. The move towards a Hindu state in India has become enforced public policy with new anti-conversion laws. As the West promotes its secular, lawless, and godless agenda, Christians are increasingly maligned as enemies of civilization. While Christianity is discarded as being as unnecessary as wisdom teeth, a beast has surfaced with teeth that grind to a pulp any vestiges of piety.

Jesus came to destroy the works of the devil. He will do this with abrupt finality at his second coming. He restrains the nations now, ruling them with a rod of iron and destroying the works of the devil wherever and whenever his people call on his holy name.

Earnest, united, and persevering prayer is the essential countermeasure for the tide to be turned. *This kind [of evil] comes not out except by prayer* (Matthew 17:21 NJKV).

When the powers that be align with the powers beneath, we pray for the destruction of the devil's works and the confounding of his malice. We claim the conquest of the enemy won at the cross; we pray for the strong man to be bound and for captives to be released and rescued. We conquer with bold evangelism, just as *they have conquered him by the blood of the lamb and by the word of their testimony* (Revelation 12:11).

Beholding the formidable array of enemies pitted against us, we could easily be overwhelmed. As Paul asks, *Who is sufficient for these things?* (2 Corinthians 2:16). Before we presume to engage demonic evil head-on, the first step in this battle is to engage the battle within ourselves. We must wrestle with our own weakness, sins, and failings. Luther, a great spiritual warrior, understood this: "To fight against sin is to fight against the devil, the world, and oneself. The fight against oneself is the worst fight of all."

Within our own souls or against the devil and his allies, the battle is the Lord's. Christ is armed and ready for battle, riding forth to conquer every seen and unseen foe (Revelation 19:1-6). In him, we claim his victory at the cross,

> *We are more than conquerors through him who loved us. For I am convinced that nothing can ever separate us from God's love. Neither death nor life, neither angels nor rulers ... will ever be able to separate us from the love of God that is revealed in Christ Jesus our Lord.* (Romans 8:37-39)

HOW TO PRAY

A United Prayer Against the Unholy Alliance

Holy Spirit, we are grateful for the unveiling of our eyes to see the pervasive presence and growing alliance of evil forces in the world against you and your Church. We know that this uniting of evil forces can only be overthrown by a greater gathering of prayer. We take up arms and lift our voices together to God (Acts 4:24).

Waking us to reality is the gift of your indwelling Spirit. Becoming aware of this rising unholy alliance prepares us for the battles ahead. Forewarned is forearmed. Grant us eyes of faith not only to perceive this unholy alliance, but also to gather whole churches to behold and lay hold of our exalted Lord in his present state of power and glory.

We know Savior that you are not distressed by the vast hordes of seen and unseen evil; you are King of Kings and Lord of Lords. We confess and appropriate your sovereign rule and reign over unseen evil and all the tumultuous affairs of rulers and nations in our world today. Bring us together that we might unite and boldly stand our ground in the evil day. You guarded Israel when she was captive in Babylon. Guard us and grant that we have integrity to say "no" to the seductive Babylon spirit that surrounds today. Give us holy resolve in our prayers to do battle against the demonic alliance that would destroy the earth, exterminate your church, and silence our witness. We pray all of this in the name and mediation of our Lord and Savior, Jesus Christ. Amen

TESTIMONY

Prayer Fuels Church Multiplication Amid Persecution
From the Church in India

India is infested with idols. The everyday life of a believer involves numerous interactions with demonic powers.

Ministers must be able to discern and expel spirits, yet their primary weapons are prayer and proclamation.

Persecution is a normal part of a Christian's life. There is a large vigilante movement in India that uses violence and intimidation to silence ministers of the gospel and harass new converts. Anti-conversion laws are submitted before the Indian Supreme Court even at time of writing.

At the same time, a great multiplying movement is emerging from the Christian church in India. Prayer is the heart of this movement. Jim Whittle, the India director Equipping Leaders International reports an example:

"In one village of 5,000 houses, the local church began praying 24/7 from September 1, 2022. People signed up for two-hour periods at the church building, which is never locked. There is daily prayer walking. They read Bible aloud and spend time in prayer for the nation, for revival, and for the people. The congregation is talking about the change they see in their own spiritual lives—they are thirsty for God. There have been 10 baptisms. The leaders are investigating using audio bible equipment for the less literate and recording a prayer guide.

The Indian church still has the structure of prayer in their churches, but the training will expand it and grow it into prayer cells, which are an essential part of starting new churches. The existing prayer meeting attendees become the first prayer cell leaders. Each plant has a team from the mother church that starts a cell in the target village, even if they don't live there. They meet for prayer and then prayer walking and evangelism. When there are three prayer cells, Sunday worship begins."

One year after doing Lord's Prayer training with 180 leaders in two states, Jim has seen 295 prayer cells start in one state and 150 in another. Each of the 295 leaders of one group are praying for 20 unbelievers each, and church members are each praying for five unbelievers.

CHAPTER 4

The Powers Behind the Powers that Be (Ephesians 6:13)

"Christian, dost thou see them on the holy ground,
How the powers of darkness rage thy steps around?
Christian, up and smite them, counting gain but loss,
In the strength that cometh by the holy cross.
Christian, dost thou feel them, how they work within,
Striving, tempting, luring, goading into sin?
Christian, never tremble; never be downcast;
Gird thee for the battle, watch and pray and fast.
Christian, dost thou hear them, how they speak thee fair?
"Always fast and vigil? Always watch and prayer?"
Christian, answer boldly: "While I breath I pray!"
Well I know thy trouble, O my servant true;
Thou art very weary, I was weary, too;
But that toil shall make thee someday all mine own,
At the end of sorrow shall be near my throne."

—Andrew of Crete, 7th century

There is no territory in our world that is void of God. There is no field of human endeavor that is not involved with spiritual forces- good and bad. We are all influenced by angels for good and devils for evil.

Consider how Paul describes the world of a Christian in an ordinary church. In his fourteen letters, he moves seamlessly from seen to unseen realities. Woven into the doctrines and practices of Christian life, Paul teaches about demonic realities 33 times. He refers to Satan 22 times (Romans 16:20; 1 Timothy 3:6, 7; 1 Thessalonians 3:1, 2, 5, 12, and 2:18; Ephesians 2:2 and 6:10-12; 2 Corinthians 2:11, 4:4, 4:27, 11:3, 14, 15, and 12:2; 1 Timothy 1:20, 5:15; 2 Timothy 2:26); to demons three times (Galatians 4; 1 Corinthians 10:20; 1 Timothy 4:1); to principalities, powers, and authorities five times (Colossians 1:13, 16, and 2:15; Ephesians 2:2, 3:10, and 6:12); to elemental principles of the world two times (Galatians 4:3; Colossians 2:8); and to strongholds of opposition once (1 Corinthians 10:4).

The overarching theme of biblical teaching is that Satan, his war cabinet, and his demon allies are active inciting sin in every branch of human endeavor, deceiving those who are evil, and tempting those that are righteous. Because Satan's influence is entrenched in the world, there is often collusion between the activity of evil spirits and acts of sinful people. When this happens, unseen evil agents unite with the powers that be to devise and execute malicious schemes against the Church and humankind.

In a radically contrasting perspective, at the present time we live in "the secular age."[7] We are in an era like none other.

For the first time in human history the hegemony of rulers, educators, medical, legal and marketplace leaders, hold to and operate from a strictly material view of the world. Our secular age is defined by a cosmology that excludes the supernatural. With scientific certainty, this worldview is presented as objective and free of religious superstition. The world is void of supernatural realities.

---

[7] This phrase comes from Charles Taylor's book of the same name. This is widely considered the definitive work on the rise and nature of a secular society— stressing the comprehensiveness of the secular belief system.

The physical world is called nature, not creation; spiritual problems are psychological; wickedness is miseducation; and judgements are natural disasters.

A corollary of this secular worldview is that we can fully understand the world and how it works using our reasoning powers and utilizing the instruments of science and technology. We understand the universe through various sciences; cosmological, environmental, political, social, historical, legal, medical, industrial and the science of learning and education.

The marketplace is run by the science of algorithms. News media is shaped by opinion polls. At no point in all our study and interpretation of the world and how it works is there reference to God or other supernatural reality. When Napoleon asked Laplace where God fit into his mathematical work, Laplace famously replied, "I have no need of that hypothesis."[8]

This secular perspective is profoundly anti-Christian. Spiritual warfare is only possible when believers reject this claim to objectivity and recast it as simple atheism.

We need to remember that Satan is a deceiver on a cosmic level. *He is the dragon, the deceiver of the whole world* (Revelation 12:9). *The whole world lies in the power of the evil one* (John 5:19). There are times when an entire civilization begins to believe an outright lie. Consider how Nazi Germany surrendered to the lie of Aryan supremacy. This kind of mass delusion goes beyond what can be explained by natural means. Satan is the architect of the lie, but God permits the deception as a judgment on unbelief.

The coming of the lawless one will be in accordance with how Satan works. He will use all sorts of displays of power through signs and wonders that serve the lie, and all the ways that wickedness deceives those who are perishing. They perish because they refused to love the truth and so be saved.

For this reason, God sends them a powerful delusion so that they will believe the lie and so that all will be condemned who have not believed the truth but have delighted in wickedness. (2 Thessalonians 2:9-12)

---

[8] http://hyperphysics.phy-astr.gsu.edu/hbase/index.html

When it comes to understanding the world around us, many are too concerned about the seen world, (while others are too concerned about the unseen world). A real and present danger is when we attempt to analyze the universe, human history, politics, cultural trends in arts and philosophy without reference to God or any other supernatural realities. This secular analysis leads to secular solutions. When Christian scholars analyze our world, often there is no reference to prayer and spiritual discernment. Rather than evangelize the unbeliever, we attempt to "beat them at their own game"; we try to outthink them by offering apologetics or feats of logic. This is not how enemy strongholds will be torn down.

Apologists and defenders of the faith need to open the eyes of faith and call God's people to spiritual discernment.

Consider Spiritual Realities in Political Domain

Christ is clear: *My kingdom is not of this world* (John 18:36). In all his teachings, Jesus makes only brief reference to politics and political leaders. Concerning the emperor, Jesus says *Render to Caesar the things that* are *Caesar's* (Matthew 22:21). He dismisses King Herod, saying, *Go tell that fox, "Behold, I cast out demons and perform cures today and tomorrow, and on the third day I will finish my course."* (Luke 13:32) When Pilate claims authority over him, Jesus puts him in his place: *You would have no authority over me at all unless it had been given you from above* (John 19:11). Not even the politics of the Sanhedrin are of interest to Jesus. He summarizes their power-grabbing shenanigans by saying: *"They are blind guides"* (Matthew 15:14).

At the same time, the Bible teaches that spiritual warfare is an ongoing battle with earthly ruling powers. Consider how the powers that be unite with religious rulers to conspire against Jesus: *The Pharisees went out and immediately held counsel with the Herodians against him, how to destroy him* (Mark 3:6).

Believers in persecuted countries realize the conflict between the church and state. The church is a visible institution, congregates in a physical space, has its own government, leaders, laws, and citizens. Tyrants realize that this makes the church a counterculture, a separate society, that represents a challenge to their claim to supreme and sole rule. Dictators and governments demand supreme allegiance.

This is something Christians can never submit to. Whether it is offering incense to the emperor as to a god or signing documents of loyalty to the state, believers will always pronounce their allegiance to Christ.

Imprisoned Christian pastor Wang Yi helped craft of a manifesto when Early Rain Covenant Church was experiencing persecution in China:

Only God and his word is Lord over a person's conscience. Any manmade and worldly law, mandate, or opinion cannot negate the moral responsibilities of a person's conscience before the "God Most High." (Genesis 14:19)[9]

In our missionary travels, we pray with persecuted Christians. They do not ask for the overthrow of the government, and neither do the writers of the New Testament! They pray for their leaders. Yet, all these believers pray fervently and boldly against evil— the powers beneath the powers that be.

New Testament writers encourage Christians to see beyond the visible, to engage the enemy, to discern the spirits, to be aware of Satan's schemes, to realize that *we do not wrestle against flesh and blood* (Ephesians 6:12; see also 1 Corinthians 12:10, 2 Corinthians 2:11). When we limit our advocacy, votes, and actions towards improving or replacing governing powers, without reference to the greater spiritual war we are fighting, we fail to resist the devil. When we pray and act for political and social change without reference to the unseen battle, we mistake a skirmish for the main conflict.

In contrast, fortified by the powerful promises of God, when we unite in prayer to solicit the power of Christ, Satan and his allies will be confounded. When Satan is bound, we will be able to plunder his house and take captives for Christ (Matthew 12:29). *Resist the devil, and he will flee from you* (James 4:7).

---

[9] Hannah Nation, ed., *Faithful Disobedience: Writings on Church and State from a Chinese House Church Movement* (Downers Grove, IL: IVP, 2022).

Judge Eternal, throned in splendor,
Lord of Lords and King of Kings,
With thy living fire of judgement
Purge this land of bitter things;
Solace all its wide dominion,
With the healing of thy wings.
—Henry Scott Holland, 1902

We Can Discern the Activity of Satan in the World and in the Church

Where there is oppression and injustice in the world, the cause may include human wickedness and worldly corruption, however, we can be sure that evil spirits are active beneath the powers that be. Where there are wars of conquest, we know that Satan is behind the conflict (James 3:15-17). When lies and propaganda fill the airwaves, we can be sure the father of lies is orchestrating the deception. When murderous decrees are executed against the unborn, the elderly, and the infirm, we pray militantly against the one who *was a murderer from the beginning* (John 8:44). When public propaganda incites rulers to enact policies that kill the innocent or deface the image of God, Satan is active behind the scenes. In lands where the church is persecuted and gospel proclamation outlawed, governing authorities are mere instruments in the hands of evil spirits.

Satan and his agents also worm their way into the church. Wherever sexual immorality, heresy, and idolatry are permitted in the Church, the *Lord among the lampstands* pronounces that Satan is the principal (Revelation 2 and 3). Concerning those who teach what is contrary to the gospel, they *are children of your father, the devil* (John 8:44).

When it comes to observing truth and holiness, there are necessary divisions in a church (1 Corinthians 11:19). However, when the division becomes rancorous or maintained by gossip or false witness, we can be sure that the instigators, however unconscious of the fact, are instruments of Satan. He is an accuser.

To trouble or divide a church community he finds human accusers to do his work. When a *complaint arose* between two groups in the early church, Satan intends the complaint to rip the early Church in two. The apostles use prayer and wisdom to turn this trial to advantage. On one hand, they maintain priorities: *We will devote ourselves to prayer and the ministry of the word.* On the other hand, the apostles involve all of God's people in solving the problem. The result is that seven godly deacons are chosen by the believers, and *this proposal pleased the whole group* (Acts 6:1-7 NIV).

Christ Is the Power Above All Powers

The tides of our times can only be rightly understood in relation to the rule and reign of Christ. Any analysis of human history that neglects Christ is inadequate. The person and work of Christ is at the beginning, center, and culmination of history. His abject humiliation, his triumphant resurrection, his exaltation to power, and his imminent return are the pivot points of history.

Cosmically, Christ is enthroned at the center. He declares that *all authority in heaven and earth has been given to me* (Matthew 28:18). The history and destiny of nations, empires, and their eras proceed at the pace and toward the destiny determined by his promise and decree:

> *He raised Christ from the dead and seated him at his right hand in the heavenly realms, far above all rule and authority, power and dominion, and every name that is invoked, not only in the present age but also in the one to* come. (Ephesians 1:20-21 NIV)

This very day, King Jesus is ruling all the world powers both seen and unseen. The Father is humbling the nations on behalf of the Son:

> *Sit at my right hand, until I make your enemies a footstool. The Lord sends forth from Zion his mighty scepter. Rule in the midst of your enemies! Your people will offer themselves freely on the day of your power.* (Psalm 110:1-3)

Prayer calls down Christ's ascension power into the Church and world. Invested with the power of the Holy Spirit, prayer is a weapon for demolishing of wicked fortifications:

For the weapons of our warfare are not of the flesh but have divine power to destroy strongholds. (2 Corinthians 10:4)

Jesus came to destroy the works of the devil. When Satan is attacking, he is not passive—and we must not be either! Once clearly discerned, the works of the devil can be opposed with all the force and focus of prayers against the devil himself.

We ask for God to restrain those that are evil and grant repentance. We pray for the utter destruction of Satanic schemes and cry out to God for the overthrow of seen and unseen wicked forces. *My prayer is continually against their evil deeds* (Psalm 141:5). The advances of evil will continually frustrate us if we do not pray. We must learn to pray against evil if we are to stem the tide in our day and time.

Christian prayer emerges from discerning the powers beneath the powers that be and the power above every power. Effective prayer engages all the realms—the world above and the world beneath and the world between. Martin Luther was constantly under attack from the church and under suspicion from the governing authorities. In this warfare prayer from a 1541 hymn, Luther considers all three realms:

> Lord, keep us steadfast in thy word,
> curb those who fain by craft or sword,
> Would wrest thy kingdom from thy Son,
> and set at naught all he hath done.
> Lord Jesus Christ thou power make known,
> for thou are Lord of Lords alone.
> Support us in our final strife
> and lead us out of death to life.

HOW TO PRAY

A Prayer in Light of Surrounding Cosmic Powers

Heavenly Father, you have stationed us between your ultimate power and the powers beneath. Open the eyes of our faith to see what is unseen—to perceive the schemes of the enemy behind the plots of the wicked.

On our own we are outnumbered and outgunned. Grant us the promised power of your ascended and glorified Son, who sits in power and majesty, ruling and subduing every power in heaven and earth.

As we pray and cry out to you in this hour of adversity, grant us boldness to expose the enemies' intent. Lay bare your arm and destroy the works of the devil even now. Confound, confuse, and set to rout those rulers and powers, whether men or women, who are willing instruments of the devil. In your time and way, remove the scepter of wickedness from our land, lest the righteous stretch out their hands to do wrong (Psalm 125:3). At the same time, bless all your agents—angels, godly men, women, and children as they strive against evil. Give them boldness to take a public stand for you.

In the name of the King of Kings, the one whom you have set on high over every power in this age or the age to come. Amen.

TESTIMONY

A Friend in a Very High Place
A Story of Standing Firm Under Scrutiny

We are having café-con-leche with a cancer-screening doctor in central Cuba. She operates the only cancer clinic in a large region. If this clinic were to close, vast numbers of cancer sufferers would have no access to the technology. "L" works for a few dollars a day. Unable to afford a car, she hitchhikes the several miles to the clinic. People in the area know her and always give her a ride. L is a forthright and bold Christian; on her clinic wall is a cross, and she regularly shares her faith with her patients.

She shared with us a time when two government controllers came to the clinic and interrogated her. They question her about reports that she had been talking with her patients about Jesus. Here is her story:

"Two government controllers came into our clinic to question me. They heard I was sharing my faith with patients. They couldn't fail to notice the cross on the wall. As soon as they started questioning me, I knew I was in trouble. They would not think twice about removing me from this position or even closing the clinic. I was anxious and uncertain about how to answer them. Before answering their questions, I turned around, facing the imaging technology, I offered up a prayer, "Lord, give me wisdom about what to say." As soon as I prayed, I knew how to respond.

Turning to face my questioners, I calmly and deliberately said, "I want you both to know that I have a friend in a very high place." The controllers looked at each other with apprehension. They would not dare to interfere with me if they knew I had political connections. They briefly conversed. After a minute, they blurted, "Okay, just be careful to follow the government guidelines." They left as quickly as they came."

*Dear Reader: Be encouraged you have a friend in a very high place too.

CHAPTER 5

What It Means to Take a Stand

"Stand up, stand up for Jesus, Stand in his strength alone,
The arm of flesh will fail you, You dare not trust your own:
Put on the gospel armor, Each piece put on with prayer;
Where duty calls or danger, Be never wanting there."

—George Duffield, 1858

Archimedes argued, "Give me a place to stand and a lever long enough and I will move the world." Everything in this world is transient and shifting, even more in an age when foundations are being destroyed (Psalm 11:3). On the other hand, stand with Christ, and you can move the world. The King of Kings is eternally seated at the right hand of God. From his eternally fixed throne room, he rules and subdues his enemies and guides his Church (Acts 2:33). From his resurrection to his second coming, Christ determines the direction and destiny of human history.

In the mind's eye of our collective imagination today, we picture a universe of infinite size and complexity; the vast blackness of space populated with hundreds of billions brilliant galaxies; the solitary earth an insignificant blue jewel suspended in the dark void of almost infinite space. This is the world's view of itself.

Scripture gives us a different vision. In this picture, the Lamb is on the throne and is the absolute center of all that exists.

> *Then I looked and heard the voice of many angels, numbering thousands upon thousands, and ten thousand times ten thousand. They encircled the throne and the living creatures and the elders. In a loud voice they were saying: "Worthy is the Lamb, who was slain, to receive power and wealth and wisdom and strength and honor and glory and praise!"…Then I heard every creature in heaven and on earth and under the earth and on the sea, and all that is in them, saying: "To him who sits on the throne and to the Lamb be praise and honor and glory and power, for ever and ever!* (Revelation 5:11-13 NIV)

Another scientist taught us to look at the world from a unique perspective. Albert Einstein argued that space and time are relative. There is no stationary place in the universe to provide a vantage point to view or measure the whole.

In the biblical vision, there is an absolute vantage point. It is the throne-room, and the ultimate one who measures reality is Christ. The hymn "The Lord is King" describes it well.

> The Lord is King! Lift up thy voice,
> O earth, and all ye heavens, rejoice;
> from world to world the joy shall ring,
> The Lord omnipotent is King!
> Alike pervaded by his eye
> all parts of his dominion lie:
> this world of ours and worlds unseen,
> and thin the boundary between!

By faith we stand on a Rock, and the Rock is Christ. Christ is our fortress, and his throne room is the launching point of every campaign in our long warfare. Whatever field of battle we enter, Christians are seated with the ascended, all-powerful Christ (Ephesians 2:6). In united prayer we come to the Rock.

The Christian Life is a Battle Against Evil

Some preachers avoid the military language of Scripture. This is a serious mistake. The Bible describes the Christian life in military terms. Every Christian is a soldier of the cross. Believers occupy hostile territory.

> *Be strong in the Lord and in his mighty power. Put on the whole armor of God, that you may be able to stand against scheme of the devil. For we do not wrestle against flesh and blood, but against the rulers, against the authorities, against the cosmic powers over this present darkness, against the spiritual forces of evil in the heavenly places. Therefore take up the whole armor of God, that you may be able to withstand in the evil day, and having done all, to stand firm.* (Ephesians 6:10-13)

Paul's descriptive phrase, *this present darkness,* depicts a world usurped and dominated by Satan. Five times in this brief passage, Paul reminds us that we live out the Christian life *against* a host of opponents. Wherever we are and wherever we turn, we must stand ready to engage unseen enemies. Paul speaks of a vast enemy army, heavily armed and marshalled for war, a many-layered strategic force of principalities, powers, rulers, authorities, and hosts of wickedness. Anglican theologian John Stott describes the Christian's reality:

> We all wish we could spend our lives in undisturbed tranquility, among our loved ones at home and in the fellowship of God's people. But the way of the escapist has been effectively blocked. Christians have to face the prospect of conflict with God's enemy and theirs. This is a stirring call to battle … Do you not hear the bugle and the trumpet? … We are being roused … The whole tone is martial, it is manly, it is strong.[10]

Vigilance is essential. Satan is like a hungry lion, stalking prey. (1 Peter 5:8). An apex predator, the devil preys on the vulnerable, the unsuspecting, and the isolated. Think too much about demons and you will be a fanatic; stop thinking about them and you will be dead.

---

[10] John R. W. Stott, *God's New Society: The Message of Ephesians* (Downers Grove, IL: InterVarsity Press, 1979)

Human armaments are useless in this war. Only a superior, entirely non-human strength can defend and prevail against these foes. Martin Luther penned this insight in the famous hymn, "A Mighty Fortress is Our God":

> Did we in our own strength confide,
> our striving would be losing;
> Were not the right man on our side,
> the man of God's own choosing.
> Dost ask who that may be?
> Christ Jesus it is he.
> Lord Sabbaoth his name,
> from age to age the same,
> And he must win the battle.

Unseen hosts are so vast a number that multiple layers of leadership are needed to coordinate their ancient strategy. The global powers of wickedness are called *archas* (rulers); *exousias* (authorities); *kosmokratos* (cosmic powers).

Satan's evil domain extends to global proportions. John tells us, *the whole world lies in the power of the evil one* (1 John 5:19). Satan is able to *deceive the nations* (Revelation 20:3), and he will make light work of the unsuspecting.

The devil uses human agents as his pawns. Whenever he plans an all-out assault on a nation, city, or church from within, he orchestrates an allegiance of human and demonic forces. The army under Satan's command can commandeer and conscript unguarded political authorities and powers of the world. Consider, for example, when Pharoah makes an edict to kill all the male infants (Exodus 1:15-22); when Haman requests a decree to kill all the Jews in Persia (Esther 3); when Herod tries to destroy Jesus in Bethlehem (Matthew 2); and when another Herod kills James and plans to kill Peter (Acts 12). In each of these murderous plots, a ruling authority has become Satan's agent.

Below the surface of their conscious minds, even unbelievers are aware of the presence and control of evil agents in their lives and in the world:

[The non-Christian] is all too conscious of powerful and malignant forces operating against him, which he will not hesitate to describe as demonic. ... He feels himself to be a helpless victim in a hostile cosmic order which is carrying him to a destruction which he cannot avert ... that it matters not whether he resists and is crushed at once, or acquiesces and is crushed later.[11]

Seen and unseen evil powers muster against the Church today. For example, a Christian bishop in India reports that Christians are multiplying exponentially in the Punjab region for the first time ever. He estimates that the Church has multiplied tenfold from 2011 to 2022. In response to these and other mass conversions, alarmed leaders are advocating for a Hindu nation-state. At time of writing, 12 states in India have passed anti-conversion laws. The penalty for attempting to convert a Hindu to another religion is up to five years imprisonment. At the time of this writing, even in the past weeks there have been multiple arrests.

The Nature of Our Combat

In Ephesians, Christians and Christ's Church are reminded that they *do not wrestle against flesh and blood* (6:12), and are commanded to take a stand against the hosts of evil: *Therefore, take up the whole armor of God, that you may be able to withstand in the evil day, and having done all, to stand firm* (6:13). *Stand* is a military term indicating "to hold a watch" or "stay at a post"; or "to stand and hold out in a critical position in a battlefield."

The term *wrestle* refers to hand-to-hand combat or grappling in close quarters. Christians grapples against the schemes and strategies of a clever and experienced opponent. In *Pilgrim's Progress*, John Bunyan offers a striking image of hand-to-hand combat when Christian confronts Apollyon, the prince of demons.

Apollyon broke out into a grievous rage, saying, I am an enemy to this Prince; I hate his person, his laws, and people; I am come out on purpose to withstand you.

---

[11] F. F. Bruce, *The Epistles to the Colossians, to Philemon, and to the Ephesians* (Grand Rapids, MI: Revell, 1978), 129.

Christian: Apollyon, beware what you do; for I am in the King's highway, the way of holiness; therefore, take heed to yourself.

Apollyon: Then Apollyon straddled quite over the whole breadth of the way, and said, I am void of fear in this matter: prepare yourself to die; for I swear by my infernal den, that you shall go no further; here will I spill your soul.

And with that he threw a flaming dart at his breast; but **Christian** had a shield in his hand, with which he caught it, and so prevented the danger of that. Apollyon as fast made at him, throwing darts as thick as hail; Apollyon wounded him in his head, his hand, and foot. This made Christian give a little back; Apollyon, therefore, followed his work again, and **Christian** again took courage, and resisted as manfully as he could. This sore combat lasted for above half a day, even till Christian was almost quite spent; because of his wounds, must needs grow weaker and weaker.

Then **Apollyon,** espying his opportunity, began to gather up close to Christian, and wrestling with him, gave him a dreadful fall; and with that Christian's sword flew out of his hand … while Apollyon was fetching of his last blow, thereby to make a full end of this good man.

Christian nimbly stretched out his hand for his sword, and caught it, saying, "Rejoice not against me, O mine enemy; when I fall, I shall arise." And with that gave him a deadly thrust, which made Apollyon give back, as one that had received his mortal wound. Christian perceiving that, made at him again, saying, "Nay, in all these things we are more than conquerors through him that loved us." And with that Apollyon spread forth his dragon's wings, and sped him away, that Christian for a season saw him no more.[12]

The Scriptures challenge every mature believer to move from "behind the lines" to the frontline. We are admonished to *withstand in the evil day and having done all to stand firm* (Ephesians 6:13). *Withstand* is a military technical term describing the final preparation before the actual battle.

---

[12] John Bunyan, *The Pilgrim's Progress*, "The Fourth Stage of Christian's Journey."

Having done all indicates a soldier or army having done everything the crisis demands to repel the foe and fortify his position.

The *full armor* described in Ephesians is battle gear for individual soldiers stationed and active at the battlefront. Note this is *the full armor of God*, indicating that these vestments are infused with divine power:

> *Therefore take up the whole armor of God, that you may be able to withstand in the evil day, and having done all, to stand* firm. *Stand therefore, having fastened on the belt of truth, and having put on the breastplate of righteousness, and, as shoes for your feet, having put on the readiness given by the gospel of peace. In all circumstances take up the shield of faith, with which you can extinguish all the flaming darts of the evil one; and take the helmet of salvation, and the sword of the Spirit, which is the word of God.* (Ephesians 6:13-17)

The Call to Pray

Paul ends his treatise on spiritual warfare with a call to pray:

> *Praying at all times in the Spirit, with all prayer and supplication. To that end, keep alert with all perseverance, making supplication for all the saints.* (Ephesians 6:18)

Paul charges us to be armed with prayer, to put on the gospel armor with prayer, and to pray with vigilance and urgency against our many unseen enemies. At *all times* means to pray in every season; to *keep alert* is literally to be sleepless; to pray *with all perseverance* implies a non-stop consecration to prayer.

Spiritual warfare is woven into a life of prayer and prayer is warp and woof with spiritual warfare. In Paul's 14 letters, we find 65 prayers, nine teachings on prayer, 11 exhortations to pray, and 7 prayer requests! In each prayer, he invokes the heavenly abundance of God to bless and empower his people in their battle against sin, the world, and the devil.

Considering this admonition to be vigilant in prayer, we question why many churches close prayer meetings for holiday seasons and summer vacations. Satan takes no vacations. Believers have more spare time in these seasons, so it is a great time to cultivate the fellowship of prayer. Prayer meetings can flourish in summer months and holiday seasons. In the churches we served, year after year, we found that seniors, singles, newcomers, and international students rejoice in the opportunity for fellowship and prayer any time of year and especially in the summer months and holiday seasons.

We do not pray to enter spiritual warfare—prayer *is* spiritual warfare! Win the battle in prayer and you win the war. Lose the battle in prayer and you lose the war. There is more to spiritual warfare than prayer, but there is no spiritual warfare without prayer.

Prayer and power are intimately connected. Amy Carmichael, a missionary to India from 1895 to 1951, founded the Dohnavur Mission to rescue thousands of girls and boys from sex trafficking and temple prostitution. During that period, this demonic wickedness was hidden beneath the surface of Hindu idolatry. Orphans were trafficked, and parents sold their children, both girls and boys, to priests who would sell them to patrons who abused them. Some of the younger children died from the forced sex.

It was the era of British rule, and many missionaries worked in India. Yet Carmichael felt she saw little effect despite all the activity. She attributed the lack of power to a lack of prayer. Carmichael wrote:

> Go where you will throughout this land, [of India] you will find Christian workers incessantly busy at their work … No charge of idleness can be made against us. But how is it that so much of our energy appears to be expended in vain? Holy Scripture, personal experience, the voice of conscience, all these alike suggest one answer—we have largely neglected the means which God himself has ordained for anointing from on high."[13]

---

[13] Sam Wellman, Amy Carmichael: *Selfless Servant of India* (Uhrichsville, OH: Barbour Publishing, 1998), 171.

On the mountainside, Carmichael and her fellow workers built a prayer chapel so that urgent, united, and persistent prayer could become the heart of their ministry. The Donhavur mission continues its good work today.

In our day, there are many gospel messengers who are strong in prayer. In their ministry, the Word and prayer are inseparable. The power of proclamation is proportional to the strength of the prayers that fuel it. Preaching without prayer loses its power; prayer without preaching loses its purpose.

Our Message Is Empowered

The scriptures are unashamed about the power of the gospel.

The kingdom of God does not consist talk in but in power. (1 Corinthians 4:20)

For I am not ashamed of the gospel, for it is the power of God for salvation. (Romans 1:16)

God added his testimony by signs, wonders, various acts of power. (Hebrews 2:4 NAB)

For the weapons of our warfare are not of the flesh but have divine power to destroy strongholds. (2 Corinthians 10:4)

If prayer is half the artillery of our warfare, the other half is a bold and public testimony: *They have conquered the dragon by the blood of the Lamb and the word of their testimony* (Revelation 12:11). Christians enter the heart of the battle zone when they bear witness to Christ: *We [wage war] by truthful speech, and the power of God, with weapons of righteousness for the right hand and for the left* (2 Corinthians 6:7).

The proclamation of Christ's finished work on the cross is the power that tears down strongholds. Jesus is the crux and culmination of the gospel—his divine person, his saving work, and his imminent return. If we rely on clever arguments to persuade people, we weaken the gospel. As Paul wrote, *For Christ [sent] me ... to preach the gospel, and not with words of eloquent wisdom, lest the cross be emptied of its power* (1 Corinthians 1:17).

Evangelism is simply preaching what God has revealed. God reveals his Son in the gospel, and we proclaim what he has revealed. We are messengers of revealed truth. Like ambassadors, we speak truth without interfering with the message; we pass on what we are told.

Evangelism is spiritual warfare! *The testimony of Jesus is the spirit of prophecy* (Revelation 19:10). When we faithfully proclaim Christ, the Holy Spirit wakes the seen and unseen world to the message:

> *This grace was given to preach to the Gentiles the unsearchable riches of Christ, and to bring to light for everyone what is the plan of the mystery hidden for ages in God … so that through the church the manifold wisdom of God might now be made known to the rulers and authorities in the heavenly places.* (Ephesians 3:8-10)

I have often experienced this powerful prompting to witness in my own life. After several faith conversations with a Hindu friend, the Spirit prompted me, "John, it is time to move the conversation to Jesus." I obeyed and we entered a deep discussion about Jesus finished work on the cross. I was able to fully preach the gospel.

Public evangelism is the Maginot Line of our warfare—where the battle rages most fierce. Pain and suffering often precedes harvest.

> *Rejoicing that they were counted worthy to suffer dishonor for the name…And every day in the temple and from house to house, they did not cease teaching and preaching that the Christ is Jesus.* (Acts 5:41,42)

Knowing to expect suffering prepares us for the inevitable rejection of our message by the world. We must examine our motives when we fail to make a public stand for Jesus. Our silence is compliance—a combination of unbelief and fear.

HOW TO PRAY

A Prayer for When You Need to Take a Stand

Heavenly Father, I want to move from the pew to the field of battle. You have opened my eyes and made it clear to me that your people are in a continual battle, and I am a conscript, commanded to take a stand and "toe the line."

Lord Jesus, gather your people in prayer; unite our hearts and voices in a common cry for you to vindicate your name and to break the strongholds of sin, death, and the devil.

We confess we avoid the arena of combat. We have spent no end of energy, time, and money to prepare for the battle, but we seldom engage the enemy or seek to win a neighbor or friend to Christ. We have preferred the safe cloisters of Christian fellowship to the foreboding fields of mission. We content ourselves by reading arguments against the enemy of our souls. When we do step out to share our faith, we have used reasoned arguments but have failed to warn them of coming judgment or invited them to consider Jesus. Forgive us, Lord, for our fear and trepidation.

Holy Spirit, grant us your power and holy resolve to enter the fray; to risk our lives and reputation as our Savior did; to give up the fleeting pleasures of prosperity for the greater treasure of knowing you and making you known. Lord fill us with the Holy Spirit that wakened your Church from the beginning and repeatedly since that day.

We ask all of these things in the name of the only Son of God. Amen.

TESTIMONY

Rhythms of Fasting Fuel Church Vitality
Reflections on Africa's Discipline of Prayer

Raphael Donkor is a pastor in Vancouver, BC. He moved to Canada from Ghana and has reflected on the vastly different approaches to prayer and fasting when he compares North America and Africa. Here are some of his thoughts:

"One of the distinctive marks of the Church in Africa is its annual, unfettered habit of 21 days of prayer and fasting. Prayer and fasting breaks the powers of the air and releases God's supernatural power over his people. In this way, God's people can truly become countercultural.

Although the core spiritual discipline of regular prayer and fasting may seem obvious, it is the least practiced of the spiritual disciplines in the Western Church. I believe one attribute of the Church in Africa that the West can humbly learn from is their unalloyed adherence to the habit of continual prayer and fasting.

At the beginning of every year, most churches in Africa, particularly growing, healthy churches, begin the year with 21 days of prayer and fasting in early January or February. During this time, men and women from all walks of life gather in their churches to pray after keeping a fast from 6 a.m. to 6 p.m.

Beyond this set aside time, throughout the year every member fasts and prays on Fridays, or any day that the churches choose. Some churches fast and break for communion on Wednesdays, which is also their midweek service. This habit not only renews the vitality of each member but also confers inestimable strength and power to members. In addition to this, at the beginning of every month, the first three days is devoted to prayer and fasting to welcome the new month.

Growing churches in Africa have early morning prayer sessions to start off the day. Some call it "covenant hour of prayer," others call it "early would I seek thee." These rhythms of prayer and fasting are the secret behind the growth, high praise life, and strength of the African-led churches.

Second, Western Christians seem bewildered by life and immersed in a sea of capitalism and consumerism that has robbed them of their spiritual hunger. I would like to say that fasting and prayer engenders so many benefits amongst which I will name a few. First, fasting is a spiritual catalyst to prayer. Jesus said this kind goes not but by prayer and fasting. Fasting reinforces our faith to overcome the molestations of the present age.

Jesus also said when you fast—not if you fast. This means that fasting is a routine that must be adhered to for all-round triumph. It is part of the Christian life. Fasting is also a prescription for triumphant living. Fasting enables a believer to maintain a strong spirit. Indeed, to be well-grounded in the Word, you need to eschew food and engage in plentiful reading of the Word of God during fasting. If you want to be an enviable, Satan-bashing believer, have a consistent fasting program.

Remember, Satan will strive to discourage you from this program, but you need to stay strong. Fasting looses invisible chains and sets the oppressed free.

Consider the call and promises granted to prayer and fasting in Isaiah 58:1-12. Fasting confers divine health and grants an outbreak of revelation which Isaiah calls "light"—*then your light shall break forth like the dawn, and your healing will quickly appear* (Isaiah 58:8 NIV). Fasting and prayer enable us to walk in righteousness and guarantee direct and speedy answers to prayers. Notice when Isaiah says, *Then you will call, and the LORD will answer; you will cry for help, and he will say: Here am I* (Isaiah 58:9 NIV).

Among other things, fasting and prayer grant divine access to supernatural direction: *the Lord will* guide *you always and will strengthen your frame* (Isaiah 58:11 NIV). Fasting and prayer even fire us up to do the "impossibles" by renewing us to rebuild, repair, and restore any broken walls of life (Isaiah 58:12 NIV).

The Lord also promises that in fasting he is committed to filling us with joy unspeakable, full of glory to turn down the depression and indifference in the culture and enable us ride in high places. Notice he says, *then you will find your joy in the LORD, and I will cause you to ride in triumph on the heights of the land* (Isaiah 58:14 NIV).

Anyone who gives him or herself to this rhythm will not be put to shame; these are not theoretical things but experiential truths that I practice, and which have enabled me stay upbeat in the post-Christian environment of North America. May you also find a deeper appreciation for the virtues of prayer and fasting even as you discover the power and profundity of Jesus and the Spirit's revolution."

CHAPTER 6

Guard Against Fiery Darts

Here is a call for the perseverance of the saints, those who keep the commandments of God and their faith of Jesus.

(Revelation 14:12)

We studied the tactics of the devil and how Christians are given the necessary armor to withstand Satan's attacks. In this chapter, we will examine in practice how to discern and defend against direct assaults of the devil. We will learn to recognize and overcome Satan's siege warfare and fiery darts.

Based on our four decades of pastoring and working with churches in Canada and abroad, we have often witnessed and experienced enemy hostilities. Consider this chapter a testimony of what we have learned. *We are not outwitted by Satan for we are not ignorant of his designs* (2 Corinthians 2:11).

Some Christians are skeptical when it comes to claims about demonic activity. They say they believe in the devil, but in practice, they neither understand nor practice spiritual warfare; *they have the appearance of godliness but deny its power* (2 Timothy 3:5).

We might imagine that a secular society would have fewer manifestations of evil spirits. This is strange reasoning.

Instead, we would argue that demonic activity is likely more pervasive in our secular societies than in pagan societies that acknowledge gods and demonic realities. Irreligion is the ultimate contempt for God—and nothing is more diabolical and godless. Eliminating God from public consciousness, erasing the distinction between good and evil, confusing the created order of male and female, eating away at the foundations of truth, is evidence that our secular culture is increasingly anti-God.

This anti-God outlook is a culpable ignorance. Men *suppress the truth* in unrighteousness (Romans 1:18). Heaven and earth declare his divine power and nature (Psalm 19:1-4, Romans 1:20). It takes significant conscious and subconscious effort to "study nature" instead of acknowledging the Creator. Take out God and creation becomes mere matter in motion. You can't look at a sunset through a microscope and imagine you know its power and splendor. You can't study a butterfly pinned on a canvas and tell me you understand its life and beauty.

By taking a closer look at the ministry of Jesus and the early Church, we can draw some conclusions as to whether demonic activity has lessened or increased over time.

The gospels portray Jesus and his disciples as in a continual conflict with demons. Luke summarizes Jesus' entire ministry as one miraculous deliverance after another:

God anointed Jesus of Nazareth with the Holy Spirit and with power. He went about doing good and healing all who were oppressed by the devil, for God was with him. (Acts 10:38)

Jesus destroys enemy fortifications by the power of his person and divine authority of his message. Jesus' preaching constitutes a blitzkrieg on the domain of darkness and a destruction of its fortifications. The gates of hell cannot withstand the sheer power of his presence.

When Christ invades hell, concealment becomes impossible. Demons have no choice but to rise and defend their gates.

Just as kicking a hornet's nest brings the angry insects out in the open, Christ's presence wakes the ever-present demonic forces. Subjected to Jesus' battery of warheads, they are forced to rise to the surface and engage in defensive warfare.

Any veteran of spiritual warfare can testify how the intensity of demonic opposition is in proportion to the power of Kingdom advance. One reason we do not see similar dramatic manifestations of demons in our time is because we have failed to confront hell's gates with Kingdom prayer and bold proclamation. We are not causing enough turbulence to call them out of hiding. As long as Christians remain seated in the pew, we are not waging war. We are leaving the hornet's nest alone.

This is not to say that demons are less active in times in our day. Just the opposite. When we moved into our present home, one morning we woke to find a goat's skull in the middle of our driveway. Perhaps related, we heard tell of a shaman in the area. Three followers of this false prophet, one by one divorced their partners.

However, the intensity of demonic activity should not be measured by the frequency of manifestations. Evil spirits prefer to scheme and influence hidden from view.

In the early Church, there are several instances of direct confrontation with demons: for example, the apostles reprove Simon the sorcerer; the seven sons of Sceva fail in the attempt to exorcise demons; the Philippian slave girl is delivered; and Elymus the magician is struck blind. In their travels, the apostles cast out demons as well as heal.

At the same time, Satan is an ambush predator. He is more dangerous when concealed. In most major episodes of the early Church's advance, Satan remains hidden. Reference to evil spirits is absent when the Sanhedrin gathers to forbid the apostles to preach (Acts 3, 4); when complainers within the fellowship incite division (Acts 6:1-7); when Herod initiates murder and persecution (Acts 12:1-5); or when newborn Christians in Ephesus burn all their occult and magic books (Acts 19:18-20). In each of these important battles, Satan and his fellow demons are behind the scenes orchestrating the opposition.

When Paul and others preach in pagan cities, there is a chaotic and riotous response. Following the gospel bombardment, both seen and unseen powers are wakened and come together to protect their domain. Yet, according to the record, the agents of chaos are not devils, but people—the leading citizens, idol makers, priests, and rulers of the city.

Siege Warfare

The devil is always active and scheming to overthrow the church and its message. In Revelation 2 and 3, the Lord of the Lampstands warns the seven churches that Satan is ever behind the scenes—persecuting (2:10), insinuating legalism (2:9,3:9), tempting to idolatry and sexual immorality (2:13,14,20), and sowing heretical teaching (2:6,14,15,19,24).

There are times, however, when demonic forces lash out with such sustained intensity that every discerning believer recognizes Satan is directly involved in the attack. We refer to long-term siege warfare.

When an army besieges a city, they bar every avenue of escape. They dig in, just out of reach of defensive artillery, and play a waiting game. The objective is to discourage, divide, and starve out their cornered foe. Inhabitants are helpless to defend or attack.

You know a diabolic siege is in process when peace and unity suddenly disappear, and when trials and troubles come from all sides. Satan is a brilliant strategist, and he works incognito and patiently until he is entrenched. Every effort to escape the difficulties will seem to be frustrated. When this happens, we must pray for endurance. *Here is a call for the perseverance of the saints* (Revelation 14:2).

There are signs that indicate Satan is oppressing a church. Siege warfare in a church often manifests as smoldering or rancorous divisions. Misunderstandings bubble up between family, friends, and colleagues. A root of bitterness digs in, while attempts to restore unity are frustrated. When an individual, family, or fellowship is under siege, the accuser raises up divisive people to gossip and criticize, especially targeting leaders. Discussion seems to do little good. Like trying to run through chest-deep water, progress is slow and arduous.

Siege warfare, by definition, is lengthy and hard pitched. Maintaining love and unity is a test of a congregation's character. Patience and perseverance are essential (Colossians 1:11-13). Immature people throw up their hands and walk away from the troubles, only adding to the discouragement. Paul offers a prayer for these times of trial.

> *May the God of **endurance and encouragement** grant you to live in such harmony with one another, in accord with Christ Jesus, that together you may with one voice glorify the God and Father of our Lord Jesus Christ.* (Romans 15:5-6)

Churches weak in prayer will be quickly routed. Recall how Israel was disarmed in the time of Judges. The Philistines confiscated the armories and shut down the forges. *Now there was no blacksmith to be found throughout all the land of Israel, for the Philistines said, "Lest the Hebrews make themselves swords or spears* (1 Samuel 13:19). The implication is clear; once Satan shuts down our prayer meetings, our armory has been confiscated and our blacksmith shops closed. Reigniting prayer meetings puts our blacksmiths back to work so the Church can rearm for the battle.

When we look to God in prayer, the situation is never hopeless. *God is our refuge and strength, a very present help in trouble* (Psalm 46:1). There are hidden springs for the besieged. King Hezekiah built the Pool of Siloam, fed from the Gihon Spring, to fend off a siege from the Assyrian army (2 Kings 18:17). Because the city had a continual source of fresh water, they were able to outlast the surrounding Assyrian armies. In the same way, when under siege, a church, ministry, or family will find abundant sustenance from a hidden source. When we flee to Christ for refuge and hunker down in prayer, deliverance rises like a fountain and hope floods our hearts.

Seasons of Siege Are Inevitable

Satan's attacks reveal weakness but need not be a sign of weakness! When a church or mission is following Christ with integrity, Spirit-filled activity will always draw opposition. When God's people are obedient to their calling, Satan is infuriated. When God grants conversions, Satan is offended. When former followers swear allegiance to Christ, the Devil wants them back in his domain and will seek to discourage the new converts. These babes will need incubation in fellowship and prayer to protect them.

When a church takes bold initiative to serve and engage the city, stepping out in prayer and evangelism, devils are roused to oppose and oppress. In the book of Acts, incursion into the streets and marketplace of the city is met with the same hostility as a military invasion (see Acts 19). When your church sets out to multiply prayer and accountability groups, you are kicking a hornet's nest. When leaders resolve to make disciples through prayer, before you know it, you will be under siege. A young pastor laments, "We never experienced deep troubles until we started praying!"

In the public arena, faithful churches and Christians are often under siege. Anti-evangelism policies are diabolic strongholds. When sharing the faith is outlawed for public servants, as in our Western countries, we get a taste of what believers in Communist, Hindu, or Muslim communities experience daily. We are learning what it is like to live the Christian life under siege.

Satan Enters When There Is Sin in the Camp

There are specific times when unconfessed sin opens a door and Satan enters in. *Do not give the devil a foothold* (Ephesians 4:26, 27). Habitual and unrepentant sin lowers the drawbridge for demonic assaults, torments, and enslavement. Belligerence towards correction or resistance to exhortation reveals an ungodly and rebellious attitude towards God. Leaders must be patient, courageous and willing to call divisive and rebellious people to repentance. Brothers and sisters need to do their part and *admonish one another* (Romans 15:14).

Scandalous sin amongst leaders—sexual immorality, substance abuse, or otherwise—can lead to a long-term struggle for the honor of Christ. Immediate discipline must be engaged. Public sin must be dealt with publicly, private sin privately.

When false teachers enter the flock, Satan is the one recruiting and sending these wolves. Paul writes, the Spirit expressly says that in later times some will depart from the faith by devoting

themselves to deceitful spirits and teachings of demons …
(1 Timothy 4:1-3). When false teachings are winked at,
the fortifications are already breached, and the enemy soon
entrenched. The battle to defend the truth of the faith calls
for firm, prayerful, and biblical rebuke, or the siege will be long.

When churches act in haste and choose the wrong elders, deacons, or ministry leaders, they are inviting a siege. When those who are immature, ambitious, or unschooled in the truth are appointed to lead, lengthy tribulation is in store.

Satan is strategic; he seeks to divide and undermine the leadership of a church. When leaders and shepherds cease to hold each other accountable, they become targets for the devil. The enemy goes for the lone shepherd as well as the lone sheep. Beware of nepotism. Rigorous and loving accountability among leaders is God's requisite for renewal. Leaders need to confront one another's pride, envy, ambition, or impropriety, respectfully and lovingly.

When under pressure from members in the congregation leaders often take opposing sides. When leaders divide, the church has already begun to split. If Satan can put a wedge between leaders or have them compromise, he knows he can enter the gates and conquer.

When churches receive new members without pastoral examination of their beliefs and spiritual walk, they are welcoming nominal Christians—those who are Christians in name only. They who are cool to the strong truths of Scripture will quench the spiritual fires of a church.

Satan Will Bring a Church to Its Knees if It Abandons the Great Commission

In Old Testament times, Israel refused to enter and take the Promised Land. Misled by ten fear-filled spies, they wanted to set up religion on the wrong side of the Jordan River. They did not believe that God would go before them to conquer the warring inhabitants of Canaan. They were intimidated by the enemy armies and feared for their children. Only Joshua and Caleb were courageous. Because Israel rejected God's commission, God rejected that entire generation (Numbers 13:25-14:12).

A great many who call themselves Christian today are content to pitch their tents on the wrong side of the Jordan. Intimidated by the world and seeking personal safety, they choose to be part of a church that only takes care of its members and deserts the Great Commission. Like Israel of that generation, their underlying sin is unbelief.

In his famous challenge the church, 19th-century missionary Hudson Taylor used Proverbs 24 to admonish the church of his day. Taylor was tormented by the thought that millions of Chinese people were dying without a saving knowledge of God through Christ.[14]

Rescue those being led away to death; hold back those staggering toward slaughter. If you say, "But we knew nothing about this," does not he who weighs the heart perceive it? Does not he who keeps watch over your soul know it, and will he not repay man according to his work? (Proverbs 24:11-12)

If we believe God will go before us, and weep for the fate of the lost, we will form an army of Joshuas and Calebs, who follow the Holy Spirit into the battle to rescue men, women, and children from perishing.

The Fiery Darts of the Devil

If siege is sustained opposition, fiery darts (Ephesians 6:16). are short burst attacks that can wound and penetrate the heart. Think of camouflaged snipers who take out soldiers in a battle—especially targeting officers. Spiritually speaking, unseen snipers seek to ambush a believer or church. There is no predicting when these darts will be fired. Christians must be constantly vigilant.

Arrows can fly fast and furious. Sudden and severe temptation, sexual or otherwise, can come at any time. Violent dreams and nightmares wreak havoc on sleep. Explosive and repeated anger springs out of thin air. As the Proverbs say, *a man without self-control is like a city broken into and left without walls* (Proverbs 25:28).

---

[14] Hudson Taylor, *China's Spiritual Needs and Claims* (1895), in *Perspectives on the World Christian Movement: A Reader*, 4th ed., ed. Ralph D. Winter and Steven C. Hawthorne (Pasadena, CA: William Carey Library, 2009), 323.

When Satan sends a barrage of flaming arrows prepare for challenges close to home. If Satan can't get at you, he will aim for your family and loved ones. When a believers' child begins to drift, Satan is at hand to lead them further astray.

A Christian's initial response to fiery darts should be to affirm their gospel call and not surrender the field to the enemy. When missionaries, evangelists, and church leaders are assaulted, whether by siege or fiery darts, they need to double their focus on biblical priorities: prayer, worship, Word, and witness.

The devil's intent is not only to inflict pain, but also to divert us from our calling. When division threatened, the apostles put first things first: *We will devote ourselves to prayer and to the ministry of the word* (Acts 6:4). They gave proper attention to addressing the problem but saved the best of their time and resources for Kingdom advance. This is a critical lesson. I counsel leaders under attack, "When facing enemy attack, if you have 50 hours of ministry in a week, give the best 40 hours to prayer and the word-prioritizing disciple making. Give no more than 10 hours a week, to the problem."

Five Strategies to Endure and Conquer

Despite the devil's siege and fiery darts, through the power of Christ we can endure and conquer.

First, ask God for discernment (Hebrews 5:14, 1 Corinthians 12:10, 1 John 4:1). Be aware of the enemy, discern God's hand behind it all, and you will be able to weather the storm. Satan's tempting is always God's testing. Everything that happens in a Christian's life comes from the hand of God. God uses times of siege to teach us how to fight evil, as well as to humble our pride and to grow our dependence on him.

> *Beloved, do not be surprised at the fiery trial when it comes upon you to test you, as though something strange were happening to you. But rejoice insofar as you share Christ's sufferings, that you may also rejoice and be glad when his glory is revealed.* (1 Peter 4:12-13)

Second, strengthen your prayers with Scripture. When the siege is long and bitter, or when the flurry of fiery arrows is most intense, mature believers know to retreat to a secret place to find rest and strength. *You are a hiding place for me; you preserve me from trouble; you surround me with shouts of deliverance* (Psalm 32:7). In this hiding place, we find refuge beyond the reach of harm.

Think of a granite grotto with a green clearing, supplied with water, fragrant with flowers, and abundant with fruit, carved out by Christ to shelter Christians under siege. *But the LORD has become my stronghold, and my God the rock of my refuge* (Psalm 94:22). In the heat of battle, nothing is more important for a Christian soldier than to retreat to the secret place of prayer. In "closet" prayer, a believer experiences God as a refuge and shelter.[15] I have often found strength praying through Psalm 91.

> *Whoever dwells in the shelter of the Most High will rest in the shadow of the Almighty.*
>
> *I will say of the LORD, "He is my refuge and my fortress, my God, in whom I trust." Surely he will save you from the fowler's snare and from the deadly pestilence. He will cover you with his feathers, and under his wings you will find refuge; his faithfulness will be your shield and rampart.*
>
> *You will not fear the terror of night, nor the arrow that flies by day, nor the pestilence that stalks in the darkness, nor the plague that destroys at midday. A thousand may fall at your side, ten thousand at your right hand, but it will not come near you. You will only observe with your eyes and see the punishment of the wicked.*
>
> *If you say, "The LORD is my refuge," and you make the Most High your dwelling, No harm will overtake you, no disaster will come near your tent. For he will command his angels concerning you to guard you in all your ways; You will tread on the lion and the cobra; you will trample the great lion and the serpent.*

---

[15] See David McIntyre, *The Hidden Life of Prayer*

"Because he loves me," says the LORD, *"I will rescue him;* **I will protect him***, for he acknowledges my name. He will call on me, and I will answer him; I will be with him in trouble,* **I will deliver him** *and honor him. With long life I will satisfy him and show him my salvation."* (Psalm 91 NIV)

Third, commit promises and prayers of Scripture to memory. When fiery arrows fly, the most effective defense is the Word of God (Ephesians 6:17). In Pilgrim's Progress, Christian turns the tide against Apollyon when he quotes the promises of God.

Scripture is the sword of the Spirit. The sword must be sharpened, ready, and at hand. Pray for God to guide you in choosing key passages to memorize. When I read the Bible, the Spirit speaks to me, highlighting words to put to memory. Rehearsing passages in the Psalms and the great prayers in Ephesians and Colossians has often given me strength and joy in times of severe adversity (Romans 15:30-31; Ephesians 6:19, 20; Colossians 4:2-4).

Fourth, fast and pray. When it comes to entrenched opposition, *this kind does not go out except by prayer and fasting* (Matthew 17:21 NKJV). Throughout the Bible, only earnest, urgent, and sustained prayer breaks through a demonic siege. In addition to observing regular times of fasting and prayer, I take a day of fasting and prayer when I enter a time of oppression.

Fifth, marshal a barrage of prayer from gospel friends to tear down Satan's forces. Paul solicits prayer five times: for boldness, for open doors, and for deliverance (Ephesians 6:19,20, Philippians 1:19-22, Colossians 4:2-4, 2 Thessalonians 3:1,2, Romans 15:31). Gather with other praying believers. Solicit prayer from Christians and churches outside the siege. At the time of writing this book, we regularly communicate our need for prayer to more than 200 individuals, mission, and prayer teams. We bear one another's burdens. This is like calling on a reserve army to reinforce the gates.

HOW TO PRAY

A Prayer for Times of Siege

Heavenly Father, give us eyes of faith and wisdom to discern when the accuser and enemy of our souls is at work, seeking to worm his way in, to drive a wedge between brothers and sisters. We repent when we have let our guard down in any way, neglecting your Word and allowing the devil to enter in among us.

When we endure his siege warfare, have pity on us in this time of affliction and opposition. We are weighed down by the siege of the enemy, his deceptions, divisions, and discouragements. We are often burdened by our own frailty, weakness, and sin. Give us grace to persevere in hope through this dark time and empower us to be faithful in worship and witness.

Use us even more in our brokenness that the surpassing glory may be clearly attributed to you. Grant that your light breaks through the clouds and that we may see your face. Lift us up above the storm. Lord, before all else, we take shelter in you, our Rock and our Redeemer. We find in you a hiding place from sin, want, and sorrow. Comfort us within you and within one another.

In Jesus' name we pray. Amen.

TESTIMONY

Survival and Growth Through Siege
From a Ministry Colleague in the Crucible

Every Christian leader will be attacked by the devil and tried by their personal weaknesses. Those who endure the test not only survive but also will thrive. God uses even enemy attacks to grow us. From conquered victims we become more than conquerors. What the devil means for evil, God means for good.

Mike planted a church that many would consider successful. He admits that the success led to pride and unhealthy ambition. This is the story of how Satan used siege and fiery darts to attack him from multiple sides:

"I was sitting with an elder and his wife, whom I'd known for over a decade. She began, "Pastor, I've catalogued all the people you hurt and have spoken to them. Some gave me permission to use their names, and God called me to tell everyone who will listen that you're dangerous." Within six months, the congregation was an ecclesiastical inferno. People I had served at hospital beds and family gravesides, married, vacationed with, and counseled turned with stunning ease after hearing accusations and never asking me about it. The five years of pain that followed ended up being something more sinister and ultimately more beautiful than my faults. I was in the confluence of the accuser's schemes and our Father's always benevolent but sometimes brutal providence.

The conflict the elder's wife started, became the soundtrack of the next several years. Some dear family friends joined the chorus, accusing us of being horrible people and leaving the church. They took our children's friends with them. Six staff members left over 3 years.

Things were already bad, but then they took a turn for the worse. One evening, a staff member called me weeping after he had had an illicit encounter with a woman. Eight days later another staffer's wife got on a plane and left with our former interim music director.

The church had just settled down, now this. The pain had completely overtaken me. My Sundays consisted of standing in the back of the sanctuary nervously while someone else led worship, coming up to preach, and then returning to the back.

We were now four years into this crucible, but it wasn't over. Within a year, I moderated an elders' meeting that removed my best friend's wife and son from the roles of the church for their refusal to engage us, or any gospel-centered caregiver, about a public declaration he made about himself. We and our children once again lost very dear friends. I drove home convinced that I couldn't endure congregational ministry anymore. If God was working, I couldn't see it.

Then my wife unlocked the key with the kindest wounding words anyone has ever said to me. We had developed the habit of driving around on our days off, venting our anger and pain. During one of those drives I sighed, "You know, the last five years have humbled me, just humbled me." She was quiet for a while and said, "Honey, do you think they humbled you or just discouraged you?"

Her question opened my eyes to the benevolent, beautiful invitation God was extending to me. Humility, as we know, is an elusive virtue, but I've discovered that once we're broken, pursuing it, even imperfectly, brings greater peace and joy than chasing lesser aspirations ever did. We now look back on those years as a treasure we wouldn't give up (or repeat) for the entire world."

PART II

Critical Fronts to Take a Stand

Withstand in the evil day and having done all, to stand firm.

(Ephesians 6:13)

In Chapters 1 through 6, we sought to discern the big picture of spiritual warfare. We are now aware of the major combatants in the strife.

In Chapters 7 and 8 we will examine the comprehensive assaults from within and without the church. We learn to beware the ever-present Sanhedrin, and then to stand against the growing lawlessness of our time. For the latter, we will review Paul's teaching on the man of lawlessness in 2 Thessalonians.

In Chapter 9 we examine what might be the severest trial in our warfare that is sifting. Think of Job who was ground down by Satan in the form of accusing friends. Or Peter, who was sifted by Satan to purify his faith and purge his sin. Sifting is often at the agency of Satan but always with the sovereign will and purpose of God.

In Chapter 10, we do a deep dive into the turbulent waters of digital technology and the internet. What does it mean to live in a world of electronic images and how does this relate to our spiritual warfare against idols? While many have surrendered to the powerful forces of electronic media, Christ expects and requires stout hearted resistance and extreme caution when we make use of the internet and other electronic, digital, gaming, and social technologies. In prayer and by the power of the Spirit, this domain can be made subject to Christ.

In Chapter 11, we turn the page towards the greatest privilege that comes through our battles with evil—entering into the fellowship of Christ's sufferings.

CHAPTER 7

Beware the Sanhedrin Within

"Leadership without ministry is just a Sanhedrin."

—Dr. Hugh Brom, addressing our seminary class, Spring 1984

Jesus went through all the cities and villages, teaching in their synagogues and proclaiming the gospel of the kingdom… When he saw the crowds, he had compassion for them because they were harassed and helpless, like sheep without a shepherd.

(Matthew 9:35)

Do you love me?... Feed my sheep.

(John 21:17)

Who Were the Sanhedrin?

The Sanhedrin was the supreme political and religious body of Israel. It consisted of 71 leaders, the Sadducees, Pharisees and elders of the people, and was presided over by the High Priest. Also mentioned in their "band" was the retinue of Herod, also known as the "Herodians." Lawyers, called scribes, or experts in the Law, are also indicted by Christ as part of this brood (Luke 12:45-52). The Sanhedrin convened every day to regulate the temple affairs and scrutinize the practices of the people.

This alliance was Christ's most inveterate opponent from the beginning of his ministry until his death on the cross. From the outset of his ministry, when Jesus heals a cripple on the Sabbath, the Pharisees intend to destroy him (Mark 3:6). At the conclusion of his life, the Sanhedrin banded together as a conspiratorial whole. They allied with the demon-possessed Judas (Luke 22:3); set forth false witnesses; condemned Jesus without due process; and convinced the people and Pilate to crucify him— even though Jewish law did not provide for capital punishment. Not content to rid the world of Christ, they wanted to destroy, shame, and execrate him. Our aim is to discern where the Sanhedrin survives today and to identify, expose, and oppose them, as did Christ in the gospels.

Jesus Overthrows the Sanhedrin

Jesus' cleansing of the temple was a revolt against the Sanhedrin order. His flurry of whip and cords was a revolution, fulfilling the forewarned promise of God to purify the people of God.

> *"I will send my messenger ... Then suddenly the Lord you are seeking will come to his temple; the messenger of the covenant, whom you desire, will come," says the Lord Almighty. But who can endure the day of his coming? Who can stand when he appears? For he will be like a refiner's fire or a launderer's soap. He will sit as a refiner and purifier of silver; he will purify the Levites and refine them like gold and silver.* (Malachi 3:1-3 NIV)

Several practices of the Sanhedrin occasioned Jesus' fury. The entire system evidenced a contempt for the common people and especially foreigners. The priests, Pharisees, and scribes occupied the temple as if they owned it. They commercialized the sacrificial system, turning the courts from a holy place to a marketplace for personal gain. They made the temple a hideout for their thievery—*a den of robbers*.

Rather than build the promised house of prayer for the nations (Isaiah 56:7), the Sanhedrin cordoned off Gentile seekers, put them through a costly market of money exchange to buy sacrifices—

fleeced them while at the same time refusing to even touch or speak with them. These gentiles were not rank pagans; they were true seekers of God. This was "anti-hospitality" in direct opposition to the free offer of God for all who thirst for salvation. By ghettoizing the Gentiles, the rulers of Israel abandoned the gospel of God.

Christ rejects the ways of the Sanhedrin to make way for servant leadership, a life of prayer, and the free offer of the gospel:

And Jesus entered the temple and drove out all who sold and bought in the temple, and he overturned the tables of the money-changers and the seats of those who sold pigeons. He said to them, "It is written, 'My house shall be called a house of prayer,' but you make it a den of robbers." (Matthew 21:12-13)

This act of judgment of the old order is at the same time a promise of a new order. Immediately following the cleansing, Jesus goes into the temple. He welcomes the blind and lame and heals them of their diseases. This just Savior is a kind Savior. While the children rejoice in Jesus' healings of the people, the religious establishment grind their teeth:

And the blind and the lame came to him at the temple, and he healed them. But when the chief priests and the scribes saw the wonderful things that he did and the children shouting in the temple courts, "Hosanna to the Son of David," they were indignant. (Matthew 21:14-15)

The Woes and Sentence

Later Jesus denounces the Sanhedrin and summarizes their felonies in Matthew 23:

1. *They preach, but do not practice:* Though they "sit in Moses' seat," instead of helping the needy, they lay heavy burdens on people (23:3).

2. They display their good works for praise; *they do their deeds to be seen by others* (23:5).

3. They live for the privileges of power. They love the places of honor… and being called rabbi by others (23:6-7).

4. Their converts are pressed into their own mold; *you make him twice as much a child of hell as yourselves* (23:15).

5. They demand detailed conformity to man-made traditions and extrapolations, giving them the same authority as the Bible. *You tithe mint and dill and cumin … and have neglected justice and mercy and faithfulness … straining out a gnat and swallowing a camel* (23:23-24).

6. Pharisees focus on external righteousness; *like whitewashed tombs which outwardly are beautiful but within are full of dead people's bones, within you are full of hypocrisy and righteousness* (23:27-28).

7. The Sanhedrin harbor murderous intent towards the prophetic word that judges them; *Therefore I send you prophets and wise men and scribes, some of whom you will kill and crucify…* (23:34).

Jesus exposed their actions as well as their words. This is why the Sanhedrin wanted to kill him. They felt Jesus was too broad in his interpretation of Scripture. He did not submit to the tradition of the elders. He often healed on the Sabbath. His disciples gleaned grain on the Sabbath (Matthew 12:1,2). Jesus painted outside the fabricated lines they had set. He taught and lived the heart of the law as well as the letter.

The Sanhedrin despised Jesus for being a "friend of sinners." He allowed the sinful woman to wash his feet with her tears and dined with Zacchaeus the tax collector. The Sanhedrin had predetermined the people Jesus ministered to were beyond the pale of God's mercy. From their perspective, these sinners deserved only judgment.

Jesus Demonstrates a Better Way

Consider the following contrasts:

- They quote tradition. Jesus quotes Scripture.
- The priests, scribes and Pharisees occupy the temple to ensure their own hegemony. Jesus enters the temple to gather and welcome outsiders.
- The Sanhedrin treat prayer as another religious duty. Jesus summarizes the entire purpose of the temple to be a house of prayer for the nations.
- These rulers exist to exclude; Jesus exists to evangelize.
- The Sanhedrin neglect the sheep; Jesus shepherds and cares for them.
- The temple powers devised detailed and arduous requirements for the people; Jesus was meek and lowly-lifting their burdens and gave them an easy yoke to bear.
- Temple leadership seeks the praise of men; Jesus evokes the praise of God.

After the cross, the Sanhedrin adds to its condemnation by continuing to oppose the Church (Acts 4:1-22, 5:17-39).

The Sanhedrin puts on a new face when they enter within the church. Throughout his missionary journeys the apostle Paul faces opposition *from "the circumcision party"* (see Acts 15:5ff).

From the beginning to the end of his ministry, Paul declares war on any who would compromise the Bible's teaching on the free grace that is evidenced in true repentance and faith.

> *Yet because of false brothers secretly brought in—who slipped in to spy out our freedom that we have in Christ Jesus, so that they might bring us into slavery—to them we did not yield in submission even for a moment.* (Galatians 2:4-5)

Paul uses imprecatory language when referring to the circumcision party. He declares that anyone preaching a *different gospel* should be accursed (Galatians 1:9), and states his wish that anyone troubling the new believers with a false gospel *would mutilate themselves* (Galatians 5:12 NLT).

Paul's antipathy to the Sanhedrin spirit is equally intense at the end of his life as it was earlier in his ministry. In Philippians, he says, *look out for the dogs, look out for the evildoers, look out for those who mutilate the flesh* (3:2).

Paul identifies the alliance of these human traditions with "elemental spirits" that utilize human rules, regulations, and extra-biblical requirements to enslave people.

If with Christ you died to the elemental spirits of the world, why, as if you were still alive in the world, do you submit to regulations—"Do not handle. Do not taste. Do not touch …"— according to human precepts and teachings? (Colossians 2:21-22)

Beware Signs of the Sanhedrin Today

This section is written to help leaders to beware of signs of the Sanhedrin. This full-blown alliance may not exist in your context, but there are early warning signs to pay heed to.

We might like to imagine the Sanhedrin is only a first-century problem—or a late medieval problem—like the incumbent religious leaders that Luther challenged with his 95 allegations. After all, no one is insisting on us becoming circumcised today. No one is requiring we pray or pay people out of purgatory.

Perhaps the Sanhedrin does not exist today. Unfortunately, this is not so. Jesus' holy message brought the Sanhedrin against him like swatting a wasp's nest. If we faithfully follow Jesus, preach his message, and pray for the advance of the Kingdom, we will rouse and rile their cousins today. The Sanhedrin is a perennial and pervasive reality in all ages of the church. The diabolic spirit of the Pharisee is always present, worming in, gaining allies, biding time, and lying low until these wolves in sheep's clothing slowly gain influence as they seek to control a church, mission, or denomination.

There Are Three Invariable Signs of the Sanhedrin in Our Midst

Narrating an event early in Jesus' ministry, this scripture contains all three:

> *Again he entered the synagogue, and a man was there with a withered hand.* ***And they watched Jesus, to see whether he would heal him on the sabbath, so they might accuse him.*** *And he said to the man with the withered hand, "Come here." And he said to them, "Is it lawful on the sabbath to do good or to do harm, to save life or to kill?" But they were silent.* ***And he looked around at them with anger, grieved at their hardness of heart,*** *and said to the man, "Stretch out your hand." He stretched it out and his hand was restored.* (Mark 3:1-5)

First, the Sanhedrin do not genuinely care about people. They measure their holiness by their exclusive consecration to laws, traditions, and doctrines. God's laws are intended to deepen our care and concern for our neighbor. The healing of the man with the withered hand shows what happens when compassion is removed: commitment to the law becomes judgmental and ugly—even hostile to Christ.

Second, Sanhedrin leaders gravitate to seats of judgment— where they can pronounce sentence on others, while remaining without censure themselves. Pharisees prefer committees and places of honor that examine others and avoid the ones that serve only to pastor and minister.

Third, Sanhedrin types hate to be criticized, questioned, or disagreed with. The very treatment they mete out to others is the same treatment they hate for themselves. The full fury of the scribes and Pharisees against Jesus was unleashed when he questioned and confounded them—exposing their hypocrisy. Consider their murderous hatred after Jesus questions them about healing on the Sabbath:

> *The Pharisees went out and immediately held counsel with the Herodians, how to destroy him.* (Mark 3:6)

Early Warning Signs

Sanhedrin pastors and elders talk about the church or ministry as if they own it. They speak as if they are the center of ministry, and the church exists and prospers because of them. Forgetting that Christ owns and is head of the church, they often use possessive pronouns such as "my church" or "my ministry." Forgetting that Jesus said; *You are not to be called rabbi, for you have one teacher* (Matthew 23:8).

In Sanhedrin cultures, evangelism and mercy ministry are neglected, sometimes grossly. Serving the outcast does not accrue capital or reputation. On one occasion, Jesus leaves the synagogues and goes to the surrounding streets. Outside their very doors, Jesus notices the neglected lonely, poor, seeking, shut-ins, lost, elderly, and infirm.

> *When he saw the crowds he had compassion on them, because they were harassed and helpless, like a sheep without a shepherd.* (Matthew 9:36)

The Sanhedrin spirit is at work within our midst when we neglect to pray for the lost, fail to befriend a needy neighbor, or refuse to take common cause with our fellow citizens against injustice. Contempt for those on the outside is evidence of the Pharisee within.

The Sanhedrin is overly concerned with money. This is an area of great danger and temptation. After 40 years of raising funds for church and ministry, I know this well! Nothing better exposes the heart of our motives than our attitude towards raising funds. Apart from constant prayer and vigilance, a concern for money betrays a protecting of ourselves and our ambitions. For ministries that focus their attention on endowments and estate planning, there is a danger of exploiting the flock: *you devour widows' houses* (Matthew 23:14 NKJV). It is easy to pollute motives by giving tributes to big donors and naming buildings or teaching chairs after them.

Hudson Taylor mobilized the poor to gather "a penny a week" for mission societies. John Wesley said, "If I die with more than five pounds in my pocket, may all men call me a thief and a robber."

The Sanhedrin is militant in self-protection. The Sanhedrin at the time of Christ had both a police force and prisons to enforce its hegemony over temple proceedings. In later history, the Church turned Sanhedrin when it resorted to military power to accomplish its ends—even forming papal armies to guard the Vatican and fight the crusades. The Inquisition, often brutal, could not have been effective in its trials and executions without a comprehensive surveillance and policing force. A similar spirit of suspicion and surveillance can be evident in how we conduct church business. Sanhedrin leaders like to examine others, but bristle when someone dares to challenge them or their views. A culture of scrutiny cannot create a culture of trust.

Sanhedrin leaders are territorial—they are all about denominations. For example, in our Reformed camp, some leaders are quick to criticize "broad evangelicals." We seek to perpetuate our own kind and our own denomination. This is the spirit of the Sanhedrin. Jesus shows a better way: *By this all people will know that you are my disciples, if you have love for one another* (John 13:35).

The Sanhedrin creates boundaries and strict requirements for entrance to ministry. They provide little assistance and training for the laity. People with average education, however faithful and godly, seldom pass muster in this elite. Admission to ministry "core" goes beyond a healthy concern for doctrine, is over selective as they rigorously police entrance to their inner circle.

Pharisees bind conscience with rigid and detailed laws, down to the *mint and dill and cumin* (Matthew 23:23). In the Catholic Church, the Sanhedrin has elevated human traditions, accumulated ex cathedra doctrines, multiplying sacraments, requiring prayers for the dead, taxing with indulgences, encouraging prayers to the saints, and the veneration of Mary. Scripture is our sole and final authority. When human traditions become Law that binds the conscience, we see the Sanhedrin at work.

Finally, the Sanhedrin practices centralized decision-making. Every important decision must be made or approved by ordained leaders. The body does not get to speak, except perhaps once a year at a congregational meeting when they are asked to affirm the decisions of the leaders. This contravenes the apostolic practice of involving the whole congregation in important planning and decisions. *And what they said pleased the whole gathering* (Acts 6:5). After a rigorous debate about how to further the mission of the Holy Spirit, we read; *Then it seemed good to the apostles and elders, with the whole church, to choose… Paul and Barnabas* (Acts 15:23).

The Better Way Today

We've spent this chapter revealing how Sanhedrin forces are still infiltrating today's Church. But how can we resist the devil in this form?

1. **Live a repentant lifestyle.** Each day, repent of your sin and seek the Holy Spirit's resolve to change. Practice personal accountability with trusted friends and leaders. These disciplines are something a Sanhedrin leader will never do.

2. **Guard the priorities of prayer and evangelism.** Leaders must respectfully and patiently challenge one another and the congregation when evangelism and prayer are neglected.

3. **Engage in acts of justice and mercy and bring others along.** Proclaim Christ's worldwide vision and promise to liberate the oppressed. Open the gates so that all nations can enter in:

   And the foreigners who join themselves to the LORD, to minister to him, to love the name of the LORD, and to be his servants, everyone who keeps the Sabbath and does not profane it, and holds fast my covenant, these I will bring to my holy mountain, and make them joyful in my house of prayer; their burnt offerings and their sacrifices will be accepted *on my altar; for my house shall be called a house of prayer for all peoples.* (Isaiah 56:6-7)

4. **Pray for leaders to be Christ-like and to embody his vision.** Ask God to raise up new Christ-like leaders. The person and vision of Jesus is what gathers and unites those who are willing to renounce the Sanhedrin order; humble revolutionaries who with prejudice and grim resolve are used by God to disrupt, dismantle, and overthrow the existing order wherever it has fallen prey to Sanhedrin forces.

In summary, in our day there are signs of the Sanhedrin appearing in many churches, denominations, and missions, seeking to worm their way in—or are already sending down roots. The particulars may differ, but the motives, mission and methods enumerated above are the same as in the first century. It is the duty of those who love the Lord, the gospel, the church, and the lost and hurting to beware of the Sanhedrin within.

A Word of Caution

I must share words of caution for those of us on guard against the signs of the Sanhedrin.

Pray. First talk to God about men before you talk with men about God. Exercise caution, wisdom, counsel, and prayer in your judgements.

Be humble. We have all been guilty of self-righteousness, misplaced judgement of others, and self-defensiveness. A mentor, Jack Miller, once told a group that there's a Pharisee in each one of us. He confessed, "I am a recovering Pharisee." What leader among us has not enjoyed the power we have over other people? How often has acclaim and popularity caused us to overlook the simple duties of loving the flock? I confess, without exaggeration, I have Pharisee characteristics in abundance.

A gospel conflict with Sanhedrin forces might bring divisions and even factions. If they become entrenched, these wolves will have garnered the support among the people. The battle will be full pitched, and there may be casualties: *There must be factions among you in order that those who are genuine among you may be recognized* (1 Corinthians 11:19).

Unity is paramount in the body. We must all be *eager to maintain the unity of the Spirit in the bond of peace* (Ephesians 4:3). On the other hand, when Sanhedrin forces steal their way into the flock, elders, and pastors are called to *guard the gospel* (2 Timothy 1:13). Good leaders fight wolves and warn the sheep not to stray. *Be shepherds of flock of God that is among you, exercising oversight* (1 Peter 5:2).

Pray for, honor, and submit to your leaders, speak the truth in love when you see discrimination, expose systemic and coercive use of power, speak against conscience-binding legislation, or policing of God's people. Do not gossip to others or incite division. Instead, pray and go to an elder with concerns. Becoming an agent of division is as serious a problem as the faults of the Sanhedrin.

HOW TO PRAY

If ever there was a good shepherd of the sheep it was Thomas Pollack. Born in 1836, he was an Anglican priest who left a stable parish to work alongside his brother Andrew in a poverty-stricken community near Birmingham, England. "Father Tom," as he was affectionately called by Anglicans and non-conformists alike, along with his brother, labored night and day amongst the poor. Pollack served for 30 years planting the seeds of a large and vibrant community, with ministry branches spreading throughout the area. Father Tom loved Christ's church—especially the children, "ragged little lambs," who followed in his train, grasping his robe, whenever he walked through the street of this parish.

Despite extreme poverty and severe opposition, the congregation grew from 30 to 3,000, with chapels throughout the district. The Pollock brothers also trained many leaders, using their scant salary to support three assistant ministers, seven lay readers, and four sisters, all on a pittance of 150 pounds a year! They started schools for 2,000 children, ministries for all kinds of men and women, particularly for the destitute and lonely.

Pollack's love for Christ, for Christ's Church, and for Christ's sheep fills this hymn and prayer:

Jesus, with thy church abide,
Be her Saviour, Lord and Guide,
While on earth her faith is tried:
We beseech thee, hear us.

Keep her life and doctrine pure;
Grant her patience to endure,
Trusting in thy promise sure:
We beseech thee, hear us.

May she one in doctrine be,
One in truth and charity,
Winning all to faith in thee:
We beseech thee, hear us.

May she guide the poor and blind,
Seek the lost until she find,
And the broken-hearted bind:
We beseech thee, hear us.

Save her love from growing cold,
Make her watchmen strong and bold,
Fence her round, thy peaceful fold:
We beseech thee, hear us.

May her lamp of truth be bright,
Bid her bear aloft its light
Through the realms of heathen night:
We beseech thee, hear us.

Arm her soldiers with the cross,
Brave to suffer toil or loss,
Counting earthly gain but dross:
We beseech thee, hear us.

May she holy triumphs win,
Overthrow the hosts of sin,
Gather all the nations in:
We beseech thee, hear us.

—Thomas Benson Pollock, *Trinity Hymnal,* 1986 edition, #27

CHAPTER 8

Beware Lawlessness Without

> "Lead us again O Akela. Lead us again O Man-cub, for we are sick of this lawlessness."
>
> —Rudyard Kipling, *The Jungle Book*

> *Everyone did what is right in his own eyes.*
>
> (Judges 21:25)

> "Humans now operate autonomously, without sensing a need to refer to either divine grace or divine truth. In the world come of age, people no longer require God as a working hypothesis, whether in science, in human affairs in general or increasingly even in religion."
>
> —Dietrich Bonhoeffer

As we have seen in the last chapter, the Sanhedrin sustained a wrong relationship to God's Law. They studied the scriptures day and night but in their conception of righteousness, the Law gained an autonomy. Keeping the letter of the Law was supreme, at least as they conceived and codified it. Rather than leading them in paths of righteousness, their obedience led them in a path away from God.

In stark contrast, we will now seek to withstand a defining feature of our age—the utter rejection of God's Law. This is what is meant by the Biblical term "lawlessness." Lawlessness does not mean anarchy. Those who reject God's Law and the penalties affixed to it, replace God's commandments with their own statutes and sanctions—often policing their regulations with severity that exceeds the thunder and lightning of Sinai.

Man's primal transgression is wanting to be like God—a god unto oneself. *You shall be like God* (Genesis 3:5). Seeking to be like God is also Satan's first sin. *You have said, "I am a god, I sit in the seat of gods."* (Ezekiel 28:2). The fall of man and devils is the consuming desire to be a law unto ourselves, free and self-determined, and ruling in uncontested power and supremacy.

Why do people reject God's Law? Is it because his rule is strict and repressive? Jesus gives another reason, *people loved darkness rather than the light because their works were evil* (John 3:19). The law is good because the commandments restrain and expose our evil intents and actions. God's laws address the entire panoply of sin and misery: idolatry, blasphemy, rebellion against authority, murder, adultery, theft, lying, envy, greed, and covetousness. In an age of lawlessness, evil accelerates unchecked.

God's laws set boundaries, like firm banks of a river, so that righteousness can flow deep and strong. The Law makes way for kindness and justice to flourish in religion, home, marriage, in marketplace, and government. *Whoever does what is true comes to the light* (John 3:20).

God's precepts and statutes set protective boundaries within which humankind can flourish. They are an expression of his holy and kind character.

> *The law of the LORD is perfect, reviving the soul.*
> *The testimony of the LORD is sure, making wise the simple.*
> *The precepts of the LORD are right, rejoicing the heart.*
> *The commandment of the LORD is radiant, enlightening the eyes.*
> *The fear of the LORD is clean, enduring forever.*
> *The rules of the LORD are true, and righteous altogether.*

*More to be desired are they than gold, even much fine gold;
Sweeter also than honey and the drippings of the honeycomb.
Moreover, by them your servant is warned; in keeping them
there is great reward.* (Psalm 19:7-11)

The Law of the Lord is embedded in our individual and social conscience. This is what makes humans distinct from all the other creatures. The Bible warns that those who reject God's commands self-erase the image of God:

For although they knew God, they did not honor him as God or give thanks to him, but they became futile in their thinking, and their foolish hearts were darkened. Claiming to be wise they became fools, and exchanged the glory of the immortal God for images ... Therefore, God gave them up in the lusts of their heart to impurity, to the dishonoring of their bodies among themselves. (Romans 1:21-24)

As long as this world remains, the Spirit is restraining every human being, warning against evil choices and guiding each one in the right path. It is a sign of judgment when God removes this restraint and leaves a person or people to their own devices.

God's declares, *My Spirit shall not strive with man forever* (Genesis 6:3 NKJV). This is the sober prelude to the damning indictment that precedes the flood: *Every intention of the thoughts of [man's] heart was only evil continually* (Genesis 6:5).

The Nature of Lawlessness

Satan is at work, but God is in control. While Satan is erasing the good, God is restraining evil. Once restraint is removed, the floodgates open and humankind is swept into the delusion that we can live life without the rule and reign of God. By dismissing God's law, humankind let loose a Pandora's box of seen and unseen evil.

Prophesying the end times, Paul refers to the man of lawlessness. Notice that this designation refers to a historical process as well as a person.

> *The man of lawlessness will oppose and will exalt himself over everything that is called God or is worshiped, so that he sets himself up in God's temple … For the secret power of lawlessness is already at work; but the one who now holds it back will continue to do so till he is taken away, then the lawless one will be revealed, whom the Lord Jesus will overthrow with the breath of his mouth and destroy by the splendor of his coming.*
> (2 Thessalonians 2:3-4, 6-8 NIV)

Whether or not the lawless one is an individual, Scripture teaches that "the man of lawlessness" refers to the final stage of humanity. Lawlessness is always gestating and will be fully birthed when humankind utterly repudiates the rule and reign of God. Satan is ever scheming to evict the consciousness of God from human society. In our age, he has largely succeeded. Nietzsche pronounced, "God is dead." The world agrees.

A spirit of lawlessness is sweeping over all the earth. With an astonishing rapidity, powers, and rulers in every field—government, legal and judicial, medical, educational, business and marketplace, and entertainment—have complied to the spirit of the age. The dominant engines of communication have lined up to promote the propaganda.

It is not that no one believes in God anymore; rather, in a secular world, man believes he can go it alone without God.

> One doesn't need to believe that the world has come of age and that all of our science and technology has actually closed the gaps in human need, whether spiritual, emotional, mental, or physical, to be compelled by the idea that humanity believes this to be true.
> As we approach a century of secular development since Bonhoeffer's claim, that "man believes he has come of age," I find it an apt description of how the modern world understands itself. As a psychological description of the secular world, Bonhoeffer's observation has me convinced.[16]

---

16 Hannah Nation, Comment Magazine, December 2023.

C.S. Lewis, in *That Hideous Strength* sounds a similar prophetic note concerning the quest for a godless autonomy:

> The time was ripe. From the point of view accepted in Hell, the whole history of our Earth had led to this moment. There was at last a chance to shake off that limitation of his powers which mercy had imposed on him as a protection from the full results of his fall. If this succeeded, Hell would at last be incarnate.

Godless Lawmakers Institute Lawless Decrees

The "man of lawlessness" is lawless only in the sense that he pays no heed to the rule and reign of Christ. *He will oppose and will exalt himself over everything that is called God or is worshiped* (2 Thessalonians 2:4 NIV).

Lawless times are not without laws. Note that Jesus describes even the rigorous law keeping Pharisees as lawless (Matthew 23:28). Rather, lawless rulers assume the role of God, multiplying "man-made" and "made for man" laws and policies. This is manifestly true in communist countries, and increasingly in Western countries. When the law of God is dismissed or denied, other laws always surface to replace them. These laws are policed with surveillance and severity. For example, Fidel Castro enacted hundreds of laws in the days after the Cuba revolution. "In its first nine months the new government enacted some fifteen hundred laws, decrees, and edicts."[17]

Peoples and nations cannot live without laws. The only question is who makes the rules and how will they be policed.

> *Can wicked rulers be allied with you, those who frame injustice by statute? They band together against the life of the righteous and condemn the innocent to death.* (Psalm 94:20-21)

> *Woe to those who decree iniquitous decrees, the writers who keep writing oppression, to turn aside the needy from justice, to rob the poor of my people from their right, that widows may be their spoil, the fatherless their prey!* (Isaiah 10:1-2)

---

[17] Ada Ferrer, *Cuba: An American History* (New York: Scribner, 2021), 318.

> *Justice is turned back, and righteousness stands far away;*
> *for truth has stumbled in the public squares, and uprightness*
> *cannot enter. Truth is lacking and he who departs from evil*
> *makes himself a prey.* (Isaiah 59:14-15)

Consider the swift rise of lawlessness in our day. We usurp the place of God who alone gives life or death when we terminate millions of unborn children. Whole nations are ridding themselves of the burden of the infirm and elderly through assisted suicide. In unrestrained lawlessness, rulers, doctors, and educators renounce our created sexual identity and assert that it is every human's right to choose their own gender. When faced with ecological disaster, we do not acknowledge a Creator, turn to any outside deity for aid, or confess our culpability to any god, rather by decree and technology we attempt to engineer a greener world. In a world that evicts God, man claims ownership over the globe, saying, "If there is no god, it is up to us to fix this mess."

Recall Jesus' parable of the vineyard. After the workers in the vineyard reject the landlord, abuse his servants and messenger, they resolve to take over the vineyard and make it their own. Echoing the parable, a lawless world represses the truth of God's ownership and our stewardship. This hostile takeover culminates in antichrist clarity: *Come, let us kill [the son] and have his inheritance* (Matthew 21:38).

A secular society casts off moral and religious hindrance to achieve mastery over the world and its people. The ends justify the means. Everyone is expected to bow before the progress of technological innovation in its many forms, whether medical, industrial, mechanical, educational, robotic, or informational.

Technological advance becomes the instrumental means of a restless humanity bent on subduing the environment and solving everything from global warming to viral plagues.

The Ideology of the Sovereign Self

To sustain this present darkness, the right of the individual has ascended to the highest perch. "Expressive individualism" is enshrined in the public square, taught at every level of education, and relentlessly promoted in news, entertainment, and social media.

Every person must now be a law unto themselves. Anyone who tries to impose their views or challenges someone's right to self-determination is coercive and oppressive. Asserting self-sovereignty has been crowned the highest virtue. However, the highest virtue has the greatest cost. Eliminating God from our thinking is the path to a meaningless life.

Aldous Huxley was a champion of this view and freely admitted the consequences. In *Ends and Means*, he described that the problem is not that we do not know the truth. We simply do not want to bow the knee and accept it.

> We had reasons for not wanting the world to have a meaning; and consequently, assumed that it had none, and was able without any difficulty to find satisfying reasons for this assumption. The philosopher who finds no meaning in the world is not concerned exclusively with a problem in pure metaphysics. He is also concerned to prove that there is no valid reason why he personally should not do as he wants to do. For myself, as no doubt for most of my friends, the philosophy of meaninglessness was essentially an instrument of liberation from a certain system of morality. We objected to the morality because it interfered with our sexual freedom. The supporters of this system claimed that it embodied the meaning—the Christian meaning, they insisted—of the world. There was one admirably simple method of confuting these people and justifying ourselves in our erotic revolt: we would deny that the world had any meaning whatever.

Buy into subjectivism and you become an ally of evil. Satan wants to be self-determined, free from any external authority or control. He despises authority. The devil hates the rule of God and considers it oppressive bondage. The devil wants to be a sovereign self—just like God. This is expressive individualism in its most diabolic form.

> *How you are fallen from heaven, O Day Star, son of Dawn!*
> *How you are cut down to the ground, you who laid the nations low!*
> *You said in your heart, "I will ascend to heaven; above the stars of God…*
> *I will make myself like the Most High."But you are brought down to Sheol."*
> (Isaiah 14:12-15)

Satan shapes the heedless into his likeness. He tempts his victim to affirm self-sovereignty. He teaches those he deceives to despise authority as he does (2 Peter 2:10). Unless restrained or delivered, those who surrender to this process eventually become *children of the devil* (John 8:44).

Lawlessness Leads to Anarchy

Every human being is in a quest for simplicity and order. However, when we turn to our own way, things become complicated and confused. Seneca captures this in *Letters from a Stoic*, writing: "Devotion to what is right is simple, devotion to what is wrong is complex and admits of infinite variations." Solomon summarizes; *The way of the wicked is like deep darkness; they do not know over what they stumble* (Proverbs 4:19).

Self-sovereignty is a deadly illusion. Being your own god is an intolerable burden for anyone, leading to an inner chaos of insecurity, uncertainty, and confusion. W.B. Yeats captures the disintegration of a world without foundations in his immortal poem, *"The Second Coming."* Written shortly after WWI, it is prophetically relevant:

> Things fall apart; the centre cannot hold;
> Mere anarchy is loosed upon the world,
> The blood-dimmed tide is loosed, and everywhere
> The ceremony of innocence is drowned;
> The best lack all conviction,
> while the worst Are full of passionate intensity.
> Surely some revelation is at hand;
> Surely the Second Coming is at hand.

Anarchy Leads to Tyranny

Drowning in the turbulent waters of subjectivism, people reach out and grasp anything that promises to keep them afloat. People abhor chaos. This is where the devil steps in. His promise of freedom leads to bondage. Led into sin, people are led into lawlessness, *Sin is lawlessness* (1 John 3:4). Committing sin leads to the tyranny of sin; *Everyone who commits sin is a slave to sin* (John 8:34).

When we separate individuals from God and the social fabric of conscience, people become ripe and ready for every form of totalitarian propaganda. C.S. Lewis issues a sober warning in *The Abolition of Man*:

> The molders of the new age will be armed with the powers of an omnicompetent state and an irresistible scientific technique: we shall get at last a race of conditioners who really can cut out all posterity in what shape they please.[18]

The Rule of Lawlessness Will Soon Come to an End

The ascendency of lawlessness is the sin-qua-non of the end of the world.

Because lawlessness will be increased, the love of many will grow cold. (Matthew 24:12)

That day will not come, unless the rebellion comes first, and the man of lawlessness is revealed. (2 Thessalonians 2:3)

Lawlessness represents the point of no return when a non-Christian world becomes most devil-like. *The coming of the lawless one is by the activity of Satan* (2 Thessalonians 2:9).

As we approach the final battle, the mystery of lawlessness will become clear (2 Thessalonians 2:7). Humankind will have become corrupt beyond repair (2 Timothy 3:1-5). Because of lawlessness, love's embers will burn to ashes (Matthew 24:12). For the sake of the Church, these wicked times will be shortened (Matthew 24:22).

---

[18] C. S. Lewis, *The Abolition of Man* (New York: Harper One, 2001), 60.

If mankind, at least in the West, continues its present course, a day of ruin will soon be upon us. The specific day and hour when Christ will destroy the man of lawlessness is not revealed to us. Yet we discern the signs of the times.

Authorities and rulers who fail to acknowledge the law of God will be treated as usurpers and rebels:

Then comes the end, when [Christ] delivers the kingdom to God the Father after destroying every rule and every authority and power. For he must reign until he has put all enemies under his feet. (1 Corinthians 15:24-25)

As Scripture foretells, all those who ignore the warnings and surrender to the spirit of lawlessness will suffer the same fate as the beast, the false prophet, Babylon, and the dragon.

The coming of the lawless one will be in accordance with how Satan works. He will use all sorts of displays of power through signs and wonders that serve the lie, and all the ways that wickedness deceives those who are perishing. They perish because they refused to love the truth and so be saved.

For this reason God sends them a powerful delusion so that they will believe the lie and so that all will be condemned who have not believed the truth but have delighted in wickedness. (2 Thessalonians 2:9-12 NIV)

Hell is a place of lawlessness. The inhabitants of that place have no workings of God's Spirit and have no remnants of God's image. Wanting to be like God, they become like the devil. Eventually the lawless find the place where they belong.

The Lord knows how to … keep the unrighteous under punishment until the day of judgment, and especially those who indulge in the lust of defiling passion and despise authority. (2 Peter 2:9-10)

Is It Too Late to Slow the Rise of Lawlessness?

All the signs are converging to a final reckoning. We are faced with a choice between revival or ruin, between repentance or Armageddon. Modern secularism is a new and "never before" phenomenon of godless and lawless intent. Until this present age, no nation or people have ever renounced their gods and idols and turned to entirely man-made laws and idols of technology.

> *Has a nation ever changed its gods? (Yet they are not gods at all.) But my people have exchanged their glorious God for worthless idols. Be appalled at this, you heavens, and shudder with great horror,"* declares the LORD. *"My people have committed two sins: They have forsaken me, the spring of living water, and have dug their own cisterns, broken cisterns that cannot hold water.* (Jeremiah 2:11-13)

The degenerative process of lawlessness is not helter-skelter. All authority in heaven and earth belongs to Jesus, but he is exercising his sovereign rule and reign over this lawlessness (Matthew 28:16). If this diabolic process continues, it is only by Christ's permission and purpose.

It is not too late for the Church to do her part in staying the coming judgment. When the seventy-two evangelists returned from "successful" preaching, healings, and exorcisms, Jesus prophesied that their power against the malice and might of the devil was invincible.

> *I saw Satan fall like lightning from heaven. Behold, I have given you authority to tread on serpents and scorpions, and over all the power of the enemy, and nothing shall hurt you.* (Luke 10:18-19)

More than ever, we need to discern the spirits, know the times, and recover the supernatural means to restrain lawlessness: urgent prayer, bold public preaching, and doing justice. Above all, Christians counter the spirit of lawlessness by being obedient to Christ. *Here is a call for the endurance of the saints, those who keep the commandments of God and their faith in Jesus* (Revelation 14:12).

If God grants it, there may yet be a great day of revival. When God's people unite to pray for revival in the Church and renewal for the world, God promises forgiveness and healing. (2 Chronicles 7:14). The moment we sincerely repent of our wickedness and pray that God will manifest his saving power, He will forgive, expel lawlessness, and *the sun of righteousness shall rise with healing in his wings* (Malachi 4:2).

HOW TO PRAY

A Prayer for Lawless Times

You, Lord, are one God—entire, holy, perfect in every attribute. There are no other gods before you and there are no other gods but you. Grant Lord that we place no false gods before you, seek to live independently of your Law, or give you lip service as if you are only one god in a pantheon of gods. Claim the sole place in our hearts, our prayers, and our worship. Almighty God, we pray you would destroy the works of Satan and his human allies who claim authority over your world, who decree laws that deny you and, with futility, would seek to wrest the rule and reign from your hands. Cause them to tremble lest they meet the same fate as pretender gods.

You have given us your just, holy, and good law to guide us in this lawless age. As we meditate, write your law on our hearts, and guide our intents and actions. According to the prayer of your only Son in the gospel of John, guard and keep us from the evil one, his lawless allies, and his schemes. In the public square, grant that prophetic and public messages expose the works of darkness and rebuke the corruption and misery of those who neglect or subvert your law. *Let your light so shine before others, so that they may see your good works and give glory to your Father who is in heaven* (Matthew 5:16). When we are reviled for our public faith, grant us the grace to persevere, turn the other cheek, and pray for our persecutors.

Sovereign Lord, we pray that you destroy the works of the devil and all the wickedness of his agents; restrain and replace those rulers and authorities who seek to commend and promote atheism, assisted suicide, abortion, sexual abandon, gender alteration, and all other outright rebellion against your holy law. We pray that you would bless those rulers and leaders who fear you and restrain those who do not.

In Jesus' name. Amen.

TESTIMONY

From Fear to Spiritual Warfare

From a Parent Wrestling in Prayer for Her Son

Gender alteration is a flashpoint of our current warfare against lawlessness. The front line is not in the debates of politicians, medical practitioners, or educators. As this testimony illustrates, the front line is in the lives of the victims, their friends, and families.

"Through the eyes of men there is so much that we have lost
as we look down the road where all the prodigals have walked

One by one the enemy has whispered lies and led them
off as slaves …"

"So starts the song *Come Alive* by Lauren Daigle. These lyrics have become a reality in our family over the last five years. We have a young adult son who has always been sensitive, kind, and awkward. He is on the autism spectrum, which brings the blessing of intellectual brilliance and the curse of challenges such as discomfort in his own body and the inability to fit into social situations.

Our son was a typical nerdy little boy fascinated by all things mechanical and technical. Yet, at eighteen years old, he was lured by the devil via the internet and by peers at university into acquiring a transgender identity. This culminated in him leaving our home and estranging himself from his family in order to medicalize and live in his identity as a woman.

One day, as I was praying for my son, when he was in his first year of university, the Holy Spirit pressed me with a crushing burden to pray against LGBTQ influences at school. A year later it became obvious that he was being influenced by the LGBTQ groups at university. He changed many things about himself in order to appear feminine. My husband and I spoke to him about these changes, stressing who he was in Christ. He just called them preferences and brushed our concerns off.

We felt paralyzed and unable to do much about these behaviors and changes. My son met with our pastor weekly for months, and they discussed these issues in the light of Scripture. The pandemic hit and brought isolation and constant access to the internet. Unbeknownst to us, our son had gone into the deep dark recesses of private transgender chat rooms, which completely hijacked his brain, heart, and mind into this cult-like world.

Two years after his first dabbling into transgender ideology, our son went to an obstetrician gynecologist who at his first visit gave him a prescription for female hormones so that he could transition into a "woman." When we discovered this, we struggled to even breathe and immediately called a friend to pray for our family. She prayed powerfully, reminding me that I was not alone and that this was a battle that the Lord himself would fight on our behalf. I fell on my knees and with my face on the floor cried out to God: Why? I felt the Lord say, in my mind, that there was a purpose in this experience that would go far beyond our son. He would use this for good, not only in our lives but also in the lives of many people.

My first lesson in this spiritual battle was that I couldn't do this battle alone. It would take an army of prayer warriors to fight this. The second lesson was that this battle was not only about my family. This was an extensive and aggressive frontal attack from the enemy against all of our children. I had to see this from God's point of view and have a Kingdom perspective as I prayed for our children.

The assurance and closeness I felt with the Lord during those first weeks quickly gave way to fear and discouragement. The enemy also whispered lies in my ear that led me to unbelief. As we saw the physical changes starting to happen in my son, who had been so masculine looking, terror and grief gripped our hearts and minds. We had told our son that if he took hormones he couldn't live at home. Seeing the enemy literally stealing his manhood, lying to him about his identity, and taking him down an irreversible path of destruction and potential death put me in a spiritual and mental state where the work of the devil was all that I could see.

Not having our son at home allowed us to see things with more clarity. We had tried to fight on behalf of my son and his peers in every possible human way. However, the more we tried to fight this battle with the weapons of the flesh, the greater the darkness encroached and the larger the enemy loomed. We felt surrounded by evil and couldn't sleep or have peace. We had night terrors about what our son might do to harm himself irreversibly and permanently.

The enemy had kept us focused on fighting earthly institutions in order to distract us from the real enemy: Satan and his demonic powers. We were not using the weapons of the Spirit to fight the powers and principalities that were behind this brutal attack. Our spiritual life suffered, and we became resentful, distracted, enraged, and defeated.

In exhaustion and desperation, I looked up and screamed at the heavens for help. The Lord guided me to his Word. Then, at one Prayer Current meeting I asked for prayer for joy. Four days later during worship at church, I felt joy bathing me. The Holy Spirit filled every cell of my body with inexplicable joy and supernatural peace. I was now equipped, refreshed, and ready to fight the spiritual battle. Ephesians 6:10-18 gave me the tools for fighting effectively. Regular perfunctory quiet times and prayers would not do. I discovered what Ephesians 6:17 means. *All kinds of prayers* included not just petition and supplication but thanksgiving, praise, and worship. These prayer actions became powerful battle tools that strengthened and encouraged me.

As I prayed for my son, the realization that this battle was about so much more than our family hit hard. I had been so focused on my pain that I had failed to see the Kingdom opportunity for why the Lord had put me in this place and at this time.

This is a battle! Though it is spiritual, we feel it in our flesh. It is wearing, wounding, and frightening. We have the scars to prove how we've been battered by the onslaught and assaults of the enemy.

Every time fear creeps in, I have learned to go to the Lord in prayer, to ask his people to pray for me, and to use the weaponry of spiritual combat—*the helmet of salvation, the shield of faith, the sword of the Spirit* (Ephesians 6:16-17).

Our unshakable hope is that the gates of hell will not prevail (Matthew 16:18). We know that our Savior will rescue and save our son in his time. I see evidence of what he is already doing in his life. The seeds of the Word that have been planted in his heart and mind, the early confessions of innocent, childlike faith spoken by him, and the prayers of God's people will not be in vain. We sing with Lauren Daigle:"

"Rescue every daughter,
bring us back the wayward son
And by Your spirit, breathe upon them,
show the world that You alone can save.
You alone can save!"

CHAPTER 9

Sifting: A Severe Pruning

Lead us not into temptation.
—Jesus

"Lord do not hold our sins against us.
Hold us against our sins."
—Kierkegaard

"Sanctification is throughout, in the whole person;
yet is imperfect in this life. There remains still some remnants
of corruption in every part; from whence arises a continual
and irreconcilable war, the flesh lusting against the Spirit,
and the Spirit against the flesh."
—Westminster Confession of Faith XIII

"He wills that I should holy be: who can withstand his will?
The counsel of his grace in me, He surely shall fulfill."
—Charles Wesley

The battle against sin is a war against Satan. Day by day, moment by moment, every believer must kill the sin within, even while enduring the suffering from without. The apostle Paul describes this inner war:

Put to death therefore what is earthly in you: sexual immorality, impurity, passion, evil desire and covetousness… you must put them all away… put on the new self, which is being renewed in knowledge after the image of its creator. (Colossians 3:5-10)

In the battle against sin, the world and the devil, a believer will pass through trials and temptations, often severe. Satan's fiery darts are also the Lords fiery trials, meant for the good of those who love him—to teach us humility and obedience. Our faith must be tested to be perfected.

The good news is that every trial comes from our Father's purposeful hand:

It is for discipline you have to endure. God is treating you as sons… He disciplines us for good that we might share his holiness. For the moment all discipline seems painful… but later it yields the peaceable fruit of righteousness. (Hebrews 12:7-11)

You have been grieved by various trials, so that the tested genuineness of your faith, more precious than gold that perishes though it is tested by fire- may be found to result in praise, glory and honor at the revelation of Jesus Christ. (1 Peter 1:6, 7)

Even crushing disappointments serve Gods' purposes.

"When through fiery trials, the pathway shall lie,
 my grace sufficient shall be thy supply.
The flames will not hurt thee, I only design
 thy dross to consume and the gold to refine."

—How Firm a Foundation

Sovereign Grace In Life's Warfare

In your battle against inner sin and outer sufferings, God's word gives you the most helpful information you can possibly have. I assure you that you will need this counsel at some point, or maybe several points in your Christian life. I speak from experience.

You may be entirely responsible for your trials, or partly, or scarcely at all. It does not matter. God is in control and is turning these trials to your growth in grace. When temptations and trials are fierce, you are not the one in control; evil people are not in control; Satan is not in control. It doesn't matter if back stabbers slander you, evil spirits accuse and attack you, or life's afflictions overwhelm you—God is 100% in control.

The Sovereign Lord will transform your trials. Like Rapunzel and the magic spinning wheel—God takes the ordinary thread of our trials and spins it into his gold.

Sifted through Sin, Sorrow, and Satan

Every believer is pruned, and dead branches cut off (John 15:1-11). Sifting, we might say, is a severe pruning. God uses sifting as a way of dealing with our most rooted sins. Sifting is a metaphor that could also be expressed as "shake someone apart" or "break a person down." The first step in the process of sifting wheat is to loosen the chaff from the edible grain, which is called threshing. The old-fashioned way to do this is to spread the wheat onto a floor made from stone, or tamped earth, and to beat it with a rod. The prophet Amos gives us an image of God shaking Israel: *For I will give the command and will shake Israel along with the other nations as grain is shaken in a sieve, yet not one true kernel will be lost* (Amos 9:9 NLT).

The grain and stocks and chaff are beaten to be separated, and then sifted through a sieve made by palm branches and leaves so that all that is left is the grain.

The Bible brings consolation, encouragement, and comfort when you, or someone you love, is called to pass through sifting. After learning the lessons of grace through a time of sifting—a period of surprising abundance and fruitfulness often follows.

Many noteworthy saints have had to go through severe sifting. Their faith was tried to the limit and purified to the utmost. Abraham was commanded to offer up his only son Isaac to prove his love to God; Joseph was sold and imprisoned both to be purified and to save his family; Jacob wrestled with the angel at the River Jabbok to test his faith; Jonah was humbled in the belly of a whale; Paul was knocked off his high horse and blinded on the road to Damascus. In each of these cases, the trial was severe, but the eventual results were miraculous.

A difficult passing, loss of a career, damaged reputation, severe illness, death of a child, betrayal, or abandonment by a spouse—all these things serve to sift a Christian to the grain of utter dependence on God and renunciation of self-reliance.

In some cases, sifting involves the direct agency of Satan.

Think of Job, whom God twice surrenders to Satan's attacks. (Job 1:6-12, 2:1-8). In Job's case, the chief instrument of trial and temptations of faith is not only the sufferings of this life, but also a relentless barrage of false accusations. Notice how Satan employs Jobs' friends to crush and accuse him.

Job is forsaken by friends. His entire life and glory of past years has been obliterated. His reputation is gone. Everything Job worked for in humble obedience is buried in midst of misrepresentation and false accusation.

Abandoned by friends and family, Job remains utterly alone to wrestle with Satan's agents. Job has no advocates, no comforters no intercessors. His heart cries out to heaven for vindication and redemption—for an Advocate and Redeemer to defend and represent him.

We are given the back story. Job is not perfect, but his so-called friends are in the wrong. Job is vindicated by God himself. We learn that Satan is always on God's leash. The devil's tempting is God's testing (Revelation 2:10).

Consider Peter's severe test: Simon, *Simon, Satan has demanded to have you, that he might sift you like wheat* (Luke 22: 31). Peter vainly boasts, *Even if I have to die with you, I will never betray you* (Matthew 26:35).

When the rooster crows a third time, Peter weeps uncontrollably and goes off to be alone to wrestle with his sin and the accusations of Satan. Peter recalls his shame and torment at the searching gaze of Jesus (Luke 22:61). What a great challenge of faith! How easy to cave into self-condemnation. Peter needs to meet Jesus as Redeemer, Advocate, and Friend.

> *For God alone my soul waits in silence, for my hope is from* him.
> *He is my rock and my salvation, my fortress; I shall not be shaken.*
> *On God rests my salvation..., my mighty rock, my refuge is God.*
> *Trust in him at all times, O people; pour out your heart before him.*
> (Psalm 62:5-7)

All of Peter's pomp and ceremony, bold claims, and pretended reputation is reduced to ashes after his threefold denial of Jesus. There is nothing left of Peter's pride. Only Jesus remains. Will Peter surrender to that searching glance of Jesus, or will he allow Christ to manifest himself as the one who has prayed for him, as the one who loves him, as the one he'll see him through this hour of trial as his redeemer and friend?

When we pray, *deliver us from evil*, being sifted by the evil one is the trial we pray to be delivered from. This is the test of faith in its purest form.

Why did Peter have to undergo so severe a test? I suggest that the faults of Peter were obvious to others, but not to Peter. His sin is hidden in plain sight. He is blind to his own pride of self. Peter's hidden sins had to be revealed for Christ to heal. The process was painful. Excavations of the soul were deep. Sifting served the purpose of rooting out the deeper sin—sins of nature—that can go ignored or undetected because they are so much part of who we are—our fallen self.

Consider Peter's presumptive and impetuous nature. Peter is always bold and always first. He is the first to repent after Jesus fills the boat with fish (Luke 5:8). Peter is quick to cry to Jesus, *Wash, not only my feet, but my head and hands as well* (John 13:9). Peter discovers the weakness of his faith when he leaps out of the boat to walk on water (Matthew 14:22-33). Peter is rebuked for trying to forestall Jesus' immanent death (Matthew 16:22). A careless Peter rises to his own defense, *"I will never betray you."*

To a degree Peter's bold and quick responses reveal a dramatic "all in" nature. He will always jump into the sea when he sees Jesus (John 21:7). There is a seed of faith present. As a sum however, his presumptive nature goes deeper than enthusiasm.

Peter's words and actions indicate a deeply rooted and independent self. It was not Peter's self that was the problem, it was his self-will. Shaking and sifting was required. At the edge of the Sea of Galilee, Jesus final words to Peter, could be interpreted this way:

"Peter, I won't ask you to jump out of the boat when you see me. I don't need you to be the first to speak your thoughts or defend your faith. I don't require you to walk on water. I need you to feed my sheep." (John 21:15ff)

There is too much Peter and not enough Jesus. Jesus has a greater plan for this beloved disciple. To utterly sanctify Peter, he had to be tested, indeed tempted beyond his ability to endure by natural bravery. Nothing less than the painful and severe chastening following his threefold denial will break and mold Peter into a new man. *We are judged that we might not be judged along with the world* (1 Corinthians 11:32).

It worked! Peter is not perfect (Galatians 2: 11), but the Peter of the epistles is far wiser, richer in words, deeper and more compassionate in counsel than the Peter of the gospels. In his letters to the churches, Peter's profound descriptions of the sanctifying process are the perhaps the most penetrating in the New Testament. Indeed, he begins his two letters on this very pastoral note. (1 Peter 1:3-9, 2 Peter 1:3-11).

Each one of us will be sifted. So deeply rooted are the sins of our nature that we often ignore them or even embrace them. When rebuked or chastened, we protest: "it's just the way I am", adding to ourselves, "they'll just have to accept that's how I am." Peter was a sharp-edged boulder. He had to be broken to become the rock he was destiny to be. Jesus did not come to make us better; he came to make us new.

Though we too must be sifted, we prevail in this promise: *He who began a good work in you shall bring it to completion at the day of Jesus Christ* (Philippians 1:6). By God's grace and power, only the grain shall remain.

Vindication and restoration is abundantly fulfilled in Job's and Peters' life. All those who endure sifting, will be richly rewarded with heaven's treasures. *After you have suffered a little while, the God of all grace, will himself restore, confirm, strengthen and establish you* (1 Peter 5:10).

HOW TO PRAY

A Prayer During Times of Sifting

Father, even while in the hour of temptation we pray, "Deliver us from the evil one." When our sins press against us, seen and unseen accusers multiply, our self-accusation threatens to overwhelm our souls. Father, in our darkness, let the light of your countenance shine upon us. Illumined by your Spirit, show us the path forward. Lord Jesus, when guilt threatens to leap upon us and pin us down, when despair threatens, grant us to lay hold of your mediation and intercession as our sure way forward and upward

> Though Satan should buffet, though trials should come,
> Let this blessed assurance control,
> That Christ has regarded my helpless estate,
> And hath shed his own blood for my soul. Amen

CHAPTER 10

Withstand Today's Idol Factory

"The heart of man is a ceaseless idol factory."

—John Calvin

*What pagans sacrifice they offer to demons and not to God.
I do not want you to be participants with demons.*

(1 Corinthians 10:20)

You turned to God from idols to serve the living and true God.

(1 Thessalonians 1:9)

Prometheus is the pagan deity who defied the gods by stealing fire from Olympus and giving it to humanity in the form of technology, knowledge, and civilization. For his overreaching, the gods Force and Violence chained Prometheus to a mountaintop, where he was destined to have his liver torn out and devoured day after day by an eagle. Our technological prowess has become a two-edged sword; one side comes from the heavens and the other comes from hell.

Apart from God, our souls are empty—in despair we grasp at the world. Whatever takes the place of God as the source of happiness, security, and meaning is an idol.

From ancient times until now, idolatry is Satan's chief strategy for diverting humanity from God. Immerse yourself in the world of idols and you enter the domain of darkness.

What the Bible calls *idols* or *images*, pagans call *gods*. Because idols are vehicles of worship, there is an inseparable connection between idols and the demons behind them. Devils desire to be worshipped as gods. *What pagans sacrifice they offer to demons and not to God* (1 Corinthians 10:20). In a powerful way, man-made images can serve the same purpose as idols. When we generate shiny, flawless, and unchanging images of beauty, celebrity, trouble-free autonomy, prosperity, leisure, nubile fertility and availability, these god-like portrayals cry out for veneration and imitation. There is a promise of blessing embedded in these depictions—ally yourself with these images, buy what they offer, and you will become like them! *Those who make them become like them; so do all who trust in them* (Psalm 115:8).

Why do I dare to tackle this immense subject? In good conscience, I could not write a book about spiritual warfare without addressing the Internet and contemporary communications media. There is great danger if we ignore this life-defining feature of a secular society.

Considering the present overwhelming digital onslaught, we might be tempted to wave a white flag. Yet leaders, parents, and pastors are grossly irresponsible if they fail to explore this world and teach those under their care how to navigate the Internet, avoid its dangers and discover its benefits.

In this chapter we will consider the Internet as an idol factory. We explore whether the Internet is a friend or foe; why we describe the World Wide Web as an idol factory; and the inseparable connection between the world of idols and the realm of demons.

The Internet: Friend or Foe?

The mighty Fraser River is 1,375 kilometers long. It flows from the west side of the Rocky Mountains to the Georgia Straight near Vancouver. The Fraser serves as a strategic corridor for transportation; it teems with bountiful salmon runs, and along its bank roam bears and deer. The surrounding hills are bearded with endless miles of evergreen forest.

The Fraser is also dangerous. Its deep, murky waters conceal treacherous undertows. In full flood, the river is a kilometer wide, navigable only by the sturdiest boats. As the Fraser winds through majestic mountains, it collapses into steep-walled narrows with rapids that shoot through granite chasms. Bounded by 90-meter granite walls, for five kilometers Hell's Gate Canyon compresses the Fraser down to a few dozen meters-—a maelstrom of waters careen and surge through the narrow passage.

"Hell's Gate" is a good name for the Internet. The World Wide Web is fast-flowing river of images and information. With self-control, surfing the web can be beneficial. At the same time, its deep waters conceal a murky chaos of vice and virtue, evil and good. We inhabit this electronic world like fish inhabit a river. Navigable water is hard to find.

The Internet was originally invented for military purposes, then expanded for communication between scientists. Only later did the Internet come to have its present widespread use. Whatever its beginnings there is much that is beneficial to this medium. Massive downloads of great music, quality literature, vital research, and important sermons and theology serve to enliven the medium with value and purpose. The Internet connects the globe. Teachers in every field and missionaries around the world can have a world-changing influence for good. For example, it used to take two weeks to visit three cities in Cuba. Now we can engage with 50 pastors and leaders from six cities at one time online.

A Legion of Dangers

Despite the benefits, dangers abound. Media spokespeople and promoters put a shiny face on digital technology. Closing one eye, they tend to point out the benefits but dismiss the downside. More sober media analysts and communications experts agree that whoever logs on will encounter a world of dangers. The heedless dive in and risk their soul.

The bigger meaning of "worldliness" is when we interpret the world through the world's media rather than judge the world through the lens of the Word. *Do not be conformed to this world but be transformed by the renewal of your mind* (Romans 12:2). A manufactured consciousness draws us away from the truth of a Christian cosmology and draws us into a world of idols.

It is not only what we seek that makes something into an idol. Idols also reveal their control by the intensity and devotion of the idolater. Those who turn to other gods always grasp for the illusionary benefit. As k.d. lang sings, "constant craving has always been." Full-blown idolatry consumes a person. Every waking moment, thought, and intent of the heart revolves around the idol. Like an addict, the spiritual, mental, and physical results are tragic. People can live without certain commodities, but they can no longer live without their smartphones. Note the panic when someone discovers they've lost their cellphone.

Consider this report from the US Center for Disease Control and Prevention. A CDC spokeswoman bluntly stated, "young people are in crisis." The crisis is especially acute among young women. As an article in *The New York Times* summarized: "Nearly three in five teenage girls felt persistent sadness in 2021… and one in three girls seriously considered attempting suicide."[19] Jonathan Haidt, author of *The Coddling of the American Mind*, paints an even starker picture: "We are now 11 years into the largest epidemic of adolescent mental illness ever recorded."[20]

Haidt points out the timing of this outbreak of anxiety, depression, and other mental health problems corresponds suspiciously with the rise of smartphones, Internet connectivity and social media apps. This technology has led to a culture-wide exchange of what he calls a "play-based childhood" for a "screen-based" one. That exchange has helped create a generation with fragile psyches unable to deal with life's challenges. One reason teen girls are especially hard-hit in this crisis is that they spend more time on social media platforms and websites that engender social and body anxiety.[21]

---

[19] https://www.nytimes.com/2023/02/13/health/teen-girls-sadness-suicide-violence.html
[20] https://www.afterbabel.com/p/mental-health-liberal-girls
[21] For example, see this article "Teen Girls spend more time on "sensitive" social media that can harm mental health, report says." https://www.foxnews.com/lifestyle/teen-girls-spend-more-time- sensitive-social-media-harm-mental-health-report

In the Greek myth, Narcissus stoops over a pond and sees his own image. He falls in love with this image of himself and can't leave the pool. Ultimately, he withers and dies looking at his own reflection. Like Narcissus, we can fall in love with the images put on the Internet. Fixing our attention on this reflection of our imagination becomes a virtual dream we may never wake from.

Images summarize, confine, hide what is beneath and within. They reduce our perception of a person or event. The outward appearance conceals an inward reality. A real person is much more than the image.

Social media images draw you in, force comparisons, inciting envy or jealousy. An experienced counsellor puts it this way: "Open the app. Reveal the gap. Feel like crap."

There is an inherent danger in image production. The danger is we begin to identify the image with the reality. In effect we confuse the reality and the image.

For example, the second commandment is about images, "You shall not make a graven image of anything on the earth or craft God with any created tool or into any created likeness." Why? The Westminster Confession states:

God is a Spirit. Infinite, eternal and unchangeable in his being, wisdom, justice, mercy and truth.

God is not a creature. God cannot be localized or reduced or contained. Therefore, all images or depictions of God are illusions, deceptions and lies. Images of God take away our worship and devotion from the true God, draw us into worshipping the image instead of the reality.

What is true of man-made depictions of God, their power to confuse reality with the image, has application to the image production on the Internet. The repetition and proliferation of images causes us to confuse reality with the picture.

Not only the images but the overall power of the medium itself draws many into the undertow and keeps them there.

Cloaked in captivating videos, podcasts and pictures, non-stop entertainment and social interaction, the Internet lures the unconscious mind. Dive in and it becomes almost impossible to escape. This river has few quiet eddies.

Marshall McLuhan was the pioneer-prophet of electronic media. He warned of "Zombiism," the permanent state of numbness for those who imbibe in electronic media and immerse themselves in its images. Users can be rendered catatonic by the unceasing acceleration and volume. The complexity of the Internet combined with its ceaseless barrage of disconnected images and information leaves most overwhelmed and helpless to fight the harmful undertow.

Mass Delusion

The Internet (and communications media in general) creates the illusion that there is normalcy and coherence to the world; that our activities, labors, and employments are a connected and purposeful part of a larger story. This is mass delusion of the first order. Even when it seems the world is falling apart, news reporters, culture shapers, policy makers, educators, and scientific experts present visual calm and share with clear-eyed commentary about random happenings in the world. Below the shimmering surface, the real-world lurches out of control: *The earth staggers like a drunken man; it sways like a hut; its transgression lies heavy upon it, and it falls and will not rise again* (Isaiah 24:20).

Creating the illusion of order in midst of chaos is the dubious achievement of our manufactured consciousness.

A thought experiment might help to clarify. Imagine if we were able to shut down the Internet and social media for five years. Freed from media-generated illusions of normalcy, we would wake to a different world. We would realize that we are surrounded by trash heaps of material and psychic waste. Like Neo's rude awakening when unplugged from the Matrix, beyond the shiny images we would open our eyes to the relentless accumulation and absurd incoherence of the world around us. Only after a few painful years would the illusion die. Once the deception was removed, we could sober up to reality.

We had an analogous experience in our own lives. Years ago, my family and I lived by a busy street in Vancouver. When we ventured outside our home, the noise of the traffic drowned out conversation, making it difficult to get to know our neighbors. One summer for two months, the thoroughfare was closed for sewer repairs. Quiet reigned. Everyone came out of hiding into the fresh air, conversations flourished, and neighbors got to know one another.

Deception and Delusion Are Satan's Stock and Trade

Unconscionable marketers and advertisers are architects of illusion. Like a dishonest used car dealer who uses spit and polish to cover up flaws and dents, these deceivers keep us from seeing what is real. Internet images are a makeover on the human enterprise, portraying a stainless, shiny array of products and presenting a radiant life of perpetual comfort and limitless joys. Put to cheerful music, these compelling ads and images are multiplied a thousand-fold daily. Is it any wonder we are captured and fixated on the illusion?

Exposing the deception reveals the architect beneath. Satan is a deceiver on a cosmic level. He is the dragon who deceives the whole world (Revelation 12:9). The whole world is under his sway (1 John 5:19). The serpent's domain is sustained by lies, deception, and schemes: *When he lies, he speaks out of his own character, for he is a liar and the father of lies* (John 8:44).

There are times when an entire civilization believes an outright lie. Consider Germany in 1940. The delusion of Aryan supremacy was not only achieved by Goebel's propaganda; Satan was the architect behind the powers that be. Now consider that Internet is infinitely more powerful than the communications technology of Nazi Germany. How much more susceptible are we to the deception and blandishments of the devil today?

The coming of the lawless one will be in accordance with how Satan works. He will use all sorts of displays of power through signs and wonders that serve the lie, and all the ways that wickedness deceives those who are perishing. They perish because they refused to love the truth and so be saved. For this reason God sends them a powerful delusion so that they will believe the lie and so that all will be condemned who have not believed the truth but have delighted in wickedness. (2 Thessalonians 2:9-12 NIV)

The World Wide Web Conceals an Idol Factory

Recently, while in Uganda, we drove past the Nile River. It is teeming with life for man and animals. I asked if people swim in it. The answer was a resolute "No." Hippos are dangerous, there are huge crocodiles, the deep calm waters hide deadly undertows, and there are many water-borne parasites and diseases in this river. Fishermen cast nets or lines and fish from the shore or from a sturdy boat. The Nile is too dangerous for swimming. The same is true of the internet. Sparing and wise use has many benefits. A general rule is: "Fish from the shore or navigate the waters in a sturdy boat. Never dive in!"

To be clear, electronic, and digital technology itself is not evil or inhabited by evil spirits. Like any idol, the problem is not material. Idols are images made of inert stone, metal, or wood. Similarly, digital technology is made up of electronic circuits. One person's advertising image is another person's idol. The "idol dimension" of the Internet lies elsewhere. John Calvin said, "The heart of man is a perpetual idol factory." Idolatry is within. The heart of the matter is a matter of the heart.

The early Church was born into a world of idols. It had been so for centuries and would continue to be for another 250 years. The advance of the gospel in the pagan world was an unceasing contest to banish the world of idols and the demons behind them.

Connecting ancient idol worship to our love affair with the Internet might seem an exaggeration, but the apostle makes a similar connection when he teaches that *greed is idolatry* (Colossians 3:5). If greed is idolatry, our overindulgent culture is surely as idolatrous as any ancient one.

In New Testament times, every citizen worshiped the gods, used graven images, and visited pagan temples. Idol worship was a household, civic, and empire-wide obligation.

Individual households had their gods and shrines along with daily rituals to honor these gods. Citizens participated in daily sacrifices and held fellowship in sacrificial meals. Craftsmen venerated guild idols and held national festivals to honor the gods of the empire. Temple building and idol manufacturing were significant drivers of the gross domestic product. Visit India today and you will find a similar idolatrous culture.

The early Church made incredible incursions into a society that was idolatrous in all its parts and practices. When a person became a Christian, they abandoned idol worship—and it cost them dearly. At the time it was widely believed that failing to honor the gods meant misfortune or even disaster for both family and community. Christians were excluded and derided for "impiety" and were charged with being atheists because they did not worship the gods.

In any age, those who turn from idols and refuse to yield to the temptations and demands of an idolatrous culture will also be persecuted. In *Pilgrim's Progress*, Christian and Faithful enter the idolatrous city called Vanity Fair. When they refuse to bow down to the city's gods, buy their wares, or participate in its revels, the entire populace forms a mob. Presided over by Judge Hate-good, Faithful is burned at the stake:

> Then they buffeted him, then they lanced his flesh with knives; after that they stoned him with stones, then pricked him with their swords and, last of all, they burned him to ashes at the stake. Thus, came Faithful to his end.

There are life and death consequences for idolaters. On the one hand, biblical warnings against idolatry focus on the personal harm and unhappiness caused by serving idols. *My people have committed two evils: they have forsaken me, the fountain of living waters, and hewed out cisterns for themselves, broken cisterns that can hold no water* (Jeremiah 2:13). Idols are a mirage that can never satisfy.

On the other hand, idolatry is a grievous offense against God. Read prophets like Hosea: idolatry betrays God at the same level as adultery in a marriage. Our God is jealous and infuriated by idolatry. The land commits *great whoredom* by forsaking the Lord for idols (Hosea 1:2).

Old Testament prophets foretell terrible judgments when the people turn to idols:

> *Thus says the Lord GOD: Repent and turn away from your idols… I send upon Jerusalem my four disastrous acts of judgment, sword, famine, wild beasts, and pestilence, to cut off from it man and beast!* (Ezekiel 14:6, 21)[22]

How to Desecrate the Idol Industry Today

The task of banishing idols is every bit as formidable today as it was in the world of the Bible. During revivals, Old Testament kings would tear down idols and shrines and put to death false prophets. Since Christ's finished work on the cross, we are commanded to tear down idolatrous strongholds with the spiritual weapons of self-denial, earnest united prayer, and bold proclamation (2 Corinthians 10:4).

It should greatly encourage us that the apostles and early Church were able to disrupt and eventually overthrow paganism and its idols. In the name of Christ and the power of the Holy Spirit, we have the same essential weaponry. *Put on the whole armour of God, that you may be able to stand against the schemes of the devil* (Ephesians 6:11). If the battle is spiritual, the weapons must be spiritual.

Seven Battlefield Practices in Our Warfare Against Idols

First, we must cultivate a life of prayer. This is a time to enjoy our face-to-face, intimate union with Christ by the Holy Spirit. (2 Corinthians 3:16-18). The supreme object of prayer is to grow deep in relationship with God. Augustine put it this way: "In prayer we increase the capacity of our heart for God's gift of himself." If Christ occupies your heart, there will be no room for idols. In contrast, idol worship is a ritualized transaction—limited to offering sacrifices, making donations, and observing meals and festivals to appease the gods or gain their favor.

---

[22] Other examples of God's wrath against idolatry and unrepentant idolaters include: Exodus 20:1-8; Deuteronomy 7:26 and 8:19; 1 Samuel 15:23; Isaiah 44:9-20; Jeremiah 19:13; Psalm 16:4; Romans 1:18, 23; 1 Corinthians 6:9; Galatians 5:19-21; and Revelation 2:14, 16, 20-22, 9:20, and 21:8

Second, discover the expulsive power of holy affections. You have an inner friend in the Holy Spirit. You can raise prayers to God, and you can also speak to the Spirit within. As you mature, your intimate prayer times will flow over into the rest of your day. The Holy Spirit is your counsellor, always alongside. He loves you with a jealous love and yearns for you to return His affections (James 4:5). It grieves the Spirit when you satiate yourself at the well of idolatry. *Pray at all times in the Spirit* (Ephesians 6:18). *Be filled with the Spirit!* (Ephesians 5:15) Enjoy his revelations. This fullness of life reveals the barrenness of every alternative:

> *Then you will defile your carved idols overlaid with silver and your gold-plated metal images. You will scatter them as unclean things. You will say to them, "Be gone!"* (Isaiah 30:22)

Third, repent of any hint of idolatry. Becoming a Christian means leaving the world of idols behind each day and forever. If your heart is fixed on approval, acquisition, achievement, or appearance, discern the idol, crush it to dust in tearful repentance, and pledge to God never to return. *If we confess our sins, he is faithful and just to forgive our us our sins and to cleanse us from all unrighteousness* (1 John 1:9). Make a habit of saying "No!" and it will become easier each time.

Fourth, exercise self-control and self-denial in the power of the Holy Spirit. Consider the plague of pornography. One reason Christians were to "flee idolatry" in New Testament times was that sexual immorality and prostitution were institutionalized in idol worship. In our day, a chief economic engine of the Internet is pornography, an industry fueled by sex trafficking. Walking in the Spirit requires that we cease preying upon others and start praying for others. *Walk in a manner worthy of the Lord, fully pleasing to him, bearing fruit in every good work and increasing in the knowledge of God* (Colossians 1:9,10).

What could happen were God to bring reformation and send revival today? For example, outlaw all pornography, and the fires of lust would cool, and the temperature would return to near normal.

It's informative to note that the first thing that the reformers did was to curtail the production of religious images and statues which had been proliferating in abundance in late medieval times. Promoting literacy, they substituted Scripture reading for viewing images. Were there to be a Spirit-given and scripture rich global revival in our time, no doubt there would be a similar movement to remove harmful images and curtail the proliferation of deceptive images by the unscrupulous idol makers of our culture.

Fifth, unplug … often! Keep the Lord's Day media free. Keeping Sabbath is a speed bump in the road of ceaseless media diversion—whether gaming, social, entertainment, or advertising. The early church observed the Lord's Day. The reformers kept Sabbath and Sunday rest became a part of a "healthy" civilization. If God would send revival and raise up a John Knox or Martin Luther today, mandating Sabbath keeping would be uppermost in the agenda of reform. We can only be set free if we habitually disconnect from communications media. Adding tech-free times in your schedule are essential.

Sixth, partake often in the sacrament of communion. While idolatry is participation with demons (1 Corinthians 10:20), the bread that we break is participation in the body of Christ (1 Corinthians 10:16). We feed on our union with Christ when we take the Lord's Supper. This consecrated practice exposes and expels idols.

Seventh, pray for and look forward to the day when every idol will be ground to dust. Those who use the Internet to destroy lives will meet their own destruction. The apostle John tells us that Jesus will destroy *the destroyers of the earth* (Revelation 11:18). We can pray boldly against Satan and all his works in anticipation of his final destruction.

Our greatest achievement, by God's grace we will be able to protect our little ones from drowning in a virtual world by keeping them in the real world. Have you noticed that the local zoo is more popular than ever? Cities are improving their displays, foliage, and enclosures in response to the demand.

One Saturday we took three of our grandchildren to the Calgary Zoo. We crammed into a gallery of families winding through the animal enclosures. Eager children were craning their necks to get a peek at a shy tiger or a baby gorilla. You would think that people would just log on and see hundreds of videos of animals in the wild. Why not? People are excited to see a live animal, even in captivity.

What is true of seeing animals in real life is also true when it comes to our children having an immediate experience of God. The more they are immersed in an unreal world of images, the more they lose their thirst for meeting God.

HOW TO PRAY

A Prayer for Deliverance from Idols

Lord Jesus, you are the one who searches mind and heart and will give to each one according to our works (Revelations 2:24). We confess that some of us have given our bodies to the world, and many of us have given our minds to the world. Some have complied and conformed to the idols of our age, and many have retreated and abandoned the world. Open our eyes to the mastermind behind today's idol factory. Give us your Spirit of grace and power to renounce the world that we might embrace it in words of grace and deeds of mercy. Amen.

TESTIMONY

The Importance of Setting Aside Time for Prayer and Fasting

My Personal Prayer Rhythms

I often disengage from the ceaseless discontent of the world. As I pray, God fills me. Like pouring water in a bottle expels the air, God's inner filling simultaneously expels the vain things that charm and captivate my soul. Being filled is the flip side of repentance.

Extended times of prayer and fasting purify my inner motives and expand my heart to love God, pray against the evil one, and intercede for Christ's Church. I have learned that extraordinary battles against seen and unseen evil must be met with extraordinary prayer. Jesus said his disciples will fast. The apostles and early Church were empowered through seasons of fasting and persevering prayer. When the Sanhedrin threatened the believers, the people muster for prayer (Acts 4:1 4:23-31). When division and contention arise, the apostles are determined to pray (Acts 6:4). When Herod began murdering apostles, many in the Church gathered in extraordinary, united prayer (Acts 12:5,12). Prior to great missionary expansion, apostles and prophets fasted and prayed (Acts 13:1-3).

Fifty years ago, in the Swiss Alps, in a community called L'Abri, I was taught to consecrate regular days of prayer and fasting to God. Ever since, I have learned to set aside days of consecrated prayer several times a year. In times of need and adversity, in church and ministry, I invite others to join in for days of prayer and fasting. Some days are scheduled, others as needed. God blesses our extended times of prayer and fasting in ways beyond regular prayer times.

Daily personal prayer is important but not sufficient when evil is entrenched. God commends his followers to join in corporate prayer: *Again I say to you, if two of you agree on earth about anything they ask, it will be done for them by my Father in heaven* (Matthew 18:19).

Consider that almost all the prayer times narrated in the book of Acts are corporate prayers, including several extended times of prayer and fasting. When we join our hands together in this way, we ascend above our present trials and afflictions. We experience what Jesus prayed just before his greatest affliction: *Father, I want those you have given me to be with me where I am* (John 17:24 NIV).

Think of taking an airplane to 3,000 feet. As you look at the world below, what seemed so big now seems so small. The world and all its problems are scaled to size.

This is what happens when I step aside for a season of prayer. I am lifted by the Holy Spirit and ascend to be present with King Jesus in his throne room. The world and all its problems scale down to size! Jesus looms larger, and my faith grows deeper. When I pray in the presence and power of Christ, good things happen. Communion with Christ takes the place of loneliness and isolation. Courage replaces fear. Hope expels despair.

I live near mountains. Travelling on a mountain highway in a winter storm I often descend into a deep fog. Visibility is zero, with the fog and blowing snow. I need to slow down so that I don't run into the car or truck in front of me. I need to go fast enough so the vehicles behind don't run into me. Yikes! It's a "white-knuckle" experience. Finally, I descend below the fog line. A stunning vista lies before me, and I can see for miles. Now I can enjoy the ride and the view.

When I consecrate myself to a day of prayer, I get a new perspective. Jesus rises like the sun to dispel the fog. Suddenly the landscape of his abundant life comes into full view. I can see the path clearly. Life moves from white-knuckle anxiety to anticipation, from dread uncertainty to bold adventure.

> *Therefore, the LORD waits to be gracious to you, and therefore he exalts himself to show mercy to you… blessed are all those who wait for him. … He will surely be gracious to you at the sound of your cry. As soon as he hears it, he answers you. Your Teacher will not hide himself anymore, but your eyes shall see your Teacher.*

And your ears shall hear a word behind you, saying,
"This is the way, walk in it," when you turn
to the right or when you turn to the left. (Isaiah 30:18-21)

When I pray for an extended time, God often gives me a spirit of prayer.

And I will pour out on the house of David and the inhabitants of Jerusalem a spirit of grace and pleas for mercy, so that, when they look on me, on him whom they have pierced, they shall mourn for him, as one mourns for an only child… On that day I will cut off the names of the idols from the land so they will be remembered no more. (Zechariah 12:10)

Through decades of ministry, I have learned that prayer begets more prayer. The increasing momentum of prayer is like a flywheel; once the initial inertia is overcome by concerted effort, the wheel accelerates with its own momentum.

Likewise, the benefits of extended times of prayer may start slowly, but once the initial inertia is overcome, prayer gains its own momentum. As the day progresses, intercession and praise move forward with greater ease."

CHAPTER 11

Blessed in the Fellowship of His Sufferings

"A holy war his servants wage, Mysteriously at strife.
The powers of heaven and hell engage,
For more than death or life."

—James Montgomery

*That I might know him and the power of his resurrection,
and may share (koinonia) in his sufferings, becoming like him
in his death, that by any means I may attain
the resurrection of the dead.*

(Philippians 3:10)

When the Adversary assaults—using fiery darts, siege, or sifting—there will be injury; there will be suffering; the wounds will be deep and even mortal. Believers often suffer the loss of what has become precious to them in this life— reputation, friendships, family relations, pleasure, and prosperity. When received by faith, these losses are the fellowship of the cross. We do not seek suffering but dare not avoid it.

Every faithful missionary discovers a direct correlation between phases of significant kingdom advance and the ensuing counterattack. The measure of kingdom advance is gauged by the severity of the backlash. When the gospel is multiplying, doors are opening, souls are being saved and leaders are multiplying, we have learned to brace ourselves for enemy hostilities. In our case, after a series of encouraging advances in Cuba, China, and Uganda, we endured a year of fierce attacks on ministry and personal fronts.

This sounds bleak, but I want to assure you—enduring suffering is worth it! A priceless treasure belongs to those who suffer. There is no greater encouragement in our battles, especially when wounded or discouraged, than to know we have fellowship in the sufferings of Christ. It is in our wars against evil that we are schooled in the cross and experience the profound immediacy of Christ's presence.

Share Warfare, Share Victory

If you share in the warfare of Christ, you share the victories of Christ. If you share in his victories, you will certainly share in his sufferings—rejections, setbacks, and sorrows. Dietrich Bonhoeffer literally lived his own words, "When Jesus bids a disciple to follow, he bids them come and die." When you die for Christ, count it all joy for you are experiencing the fellowship of his sufferings.

Participation in Christ's sufferings is more than just being a part of the same army. It is an unspeakably profound truth, as we go through cross and trials, most wonderfully we experience fellowship in his sufferings. As we bear the wounds of battle, we grow into deeper understanding and fuller participation in our intimate bond with Christ. Spiritual warfare is two sided. When you resist the devil, he will flee from you. When you draw close to Jesus, He will draw close to you.

Ponder This Great Mystery

There is an inseparable connection between the cross of Christ and the cross we bear. Taking up our cross daily is what it means to share the fellowship of his sufferings. We endure the same things He endured—without complaint or retaliation—forgiving others when they offend. Our trials will not only involve physical pain, we must also suffer our loss of place and prominence. *I will not boast except in the cross of Christ through which the world has been crucified to me, and I to the world* (Galatians 6:14).

Jesus knows and cares for your personal sufferings. Please grasp this. As you engage the enemy you come to experience what Christ suffered for you. In every aspect of your troubled life on earth, he drank to the dregs the very cup you are drinking. He took upon himself your sins, sorrows, sicknesses, and bondages that you might be forgiven, comforted, healed and set free. More than concern for your well-being, Jesus' sympathy for you is a shared endurance of your sorrows (Hebrews 4:15).

You Have Jesus' Fellowship In Your Inner Battles Against Sin

Jesus is no bystander to your sins. You might feel ashamed to share your sin with Jesus. How can you face the one you fled from in the heat of battle? Yet, in this very conflict you come to know that Jesus is *a friend of sinners*. Jesus is your friend. The indwelling Spirit of Christ will be your mediator, friend, counsellor, comforter, and advocate.

Jesus was abandoned and forsaken of God and men so that you will never be abandoned or forsaken. In the midst of trials you may cry out, *"My God, my God, why have you forsaken me?"* (Psalm 22:1-2). The Spirit replies deep within:, *I will never leave you. I will never fail you. I will never forsake you* (Deuteronomy 31:8).

What unspeakable comfort! It is not only when you suffer unjustly that you participate in his suffering. Your greatest war is the unabated battle within—against the strong remains of sin and corruption in your still fallen nature. Jesus endured a deadly war with your sin at the cross and won. Today he enters your battle to conquer sin. Jesus knows your deadly struggle. You have hope in your war against sin—a very present fellowship with Jesus.

> Jesus! What a Friend for sinners!
> Jesus! Lover of my soul;
> Friends may fail me, foes assail me,
> He, my Savior, makes me whole.
> Jesus! What a Strength in weakness!
> Let me hide myself in Him.
>
> Tempted, tried, and often failing,
> He, my Strength, my victory wins.
> Jesus! What a Help in sorrow!
> While the billows over me roll,
>
> Even when my heart is breaking,
> He, my Comfort, helps my soul.
> Jesus! I do now receive Him,
> More than all in Him I find.
> He has granted me forgiveness,
> I am His, and He is mine.
>
> —John Wilbur Chapman – 1910

Come to Understand What He Endured, and You Will Know the Fellowship of His Sufferings

Every seasoned soldier of the cross learns to connect their sufferings to the sufferings of Jesus. Your sufferings are never an accident. Whether the devil, disease, or devious men afflict you, the Author and Captain of your salvation permits and sends these trials for your good. In midst of your sorrows, you will learn to plumb the depths and ascend the heights of what Jesus has done for you at the cross. The Spirit will fill the cup of your praise as you come to understand his shames, sorrows, and losses. You will dive deeper in every prayer you pray and in every song you sing.

There Are Two Sides to Our Fellowship in Jesus' Sufferings

Jesus has fellowship in your sufferings, and you have fellowship in his sufferings. Jesus understands your sorrows and he wants you to understand his. He cares infinitely and intimately for your sorrows, and he longs for you to care for his. Jesus invites you to sympathize with his humiliations.

Jesus grieved when abandoned by his disciples at Gethsemane. When they could have prayed with him, they chose sleep. They lost touch with his suffering and agony. They let Jesus down. They did not understand or sympathize with him.

You have an opportunity to do better. You have the full picture. As his companion and friend, you are no longer detached from his agony, but weep for him. You have come to understand what he suffered and have the unspeakable honor to *watch for one hour* (Matthew 26:40). You share in the experience of his passion by taking time and prayer to identify and contemplate what he endured for you.

Read this hymn. Ask the Spirit to help you weep for Christ.

Tis midnight; and on Olive's brow
The star is dimmed that lately shone:
Tis midnight; in the garden now
The suffering Savior prays alone.
Tis midnight; and from all removed,
Emmanuel wrestles lone with fears:
E'en the disciple that he loved,
Heeds not his Master's grief and tears.
Tis midnight; and for other's guilt,
The Man of Sorrows weeps in blood:
Yet he that hath in anguish knelt.
Is not forsaken by his God.

—W.B. Tappan, 1822

Every parent wants their child to know how much they love them. Jesus wants you to experience how great his love is for you in what he suffered. Every lover wants their beloved to understand their affection. Jesus wants you to know the price of his love.

The inner reality that accompanies a great outpouring of the Holy Spirit is when God's people grieve for their Savior:

I will pour out a Spirit of prayer and supplication. They shall look on me whom they pierced and mourn for him as for his only son and weep bitterly for him as one weeps over a firstborn. (Zechariah 12:10)

Are not the most powerful experiences in your Christian life when you feel the sorrows that Christ felt? What a precious time when you take the bread and the wine, really remembering his death. The Spirit weeps and your tears flow.

There is a graphic biblical illustration of this blessed truth. God commanded Abraham to offer his son; *Take your son, your only son Isaac, whom you love…and offer him as a burnt offering on [Mount Moriah]…* Abraham obeys the command to the letter. He builds an altar, arranges the wood, and even takes up his own knife to sacrifice his only son.

What was the point of this strange command? It was for Abraham to experience the agony of the Father when He offered His one and only Son on that same mountain. *Now I know you fear God, seeing that you have not withheld your son, your only son from me* (Genesis 22:1-15). In the deepest way, Abraham experienced the fellowship of God's sufferings. Even today God calls a believer to sacrifice all that is most precious so that he or she may know the agony of the Father who sacrificed His Son at the cross.

We Suffer Death with Him and Die with Him

As his very body, corporately and individually we have communion in his death. We died with Jesus at the cross.

We died with Christ. (Romans 6:8)

I have been crucified with Christ. (Galatians 2:20)

We are renewed in the passion of Christ every time we take the bread and wine by faith. As real as the bread and wine are to the sight and touch, so real is our spiritual participation in his blood and body when we partake by faith.

> *The cup that we bless, is it not a participation in the blood of Christ? The bread we break, is it not a participation in the body of Christ?* (1 Corinthians 10:16)

Jesus wants you to remember his death—not merely to recall it. Study his death and you have communion in his sufferings.

Dying with Christ happens when you become a Christian. When born again, your death is passive—a work of the Holy Spirit received by faith. This death with Christ is given for you, once and for all. However, there is also an active and ongoing dying with Christ. You take up his cross and put to death your old nature every time you practice self-denial in your war against sin. You take up his cross when you follow him into the field of harvest and are despised and rejected by the very ones you call to salvation. In this fellowship of dying with Christ you experience his victory over death:

> *That I might know him and the power of his resurrection, and may share (koinonia) in his sufferings, becoming like him in his death, that by any means I may attain the resurrection of the dead.* (Philippians 3:10)

Paul concludes this declaration when he says, *I attain to the resurrection of the dead.* Resurrection endowment is not a given. We must attain it! A continual resurrection endowment follows our dying. Jesus' resurrection presence and power are experienced only when we willingly take up His cross. As William Burns, an early missionary to China often repeated, "No cross, no crown!" Shun the cross and we shun the resurrection. *If we died with Him we will also live with him; if we endure we will also reign with Him* (2 Timothy 2:11,12).

Jesus Suffers with You Every Day

My dad was a carpenter. He taught me how to swing a hammer and not miss. There is something deeply satisfying when you can say "I nailed it!" However, inevitably I would miss. The hammer glances off the nail and I strike my finger instead. Take my word for it—when you hit your finger with a hammer, your whole body and mind screams out in pain.

You are a member of Jesus' body. When the body suffers, so does the head. Jesus is no spectator of your sufferings as you walk through the pain. When you truly love someone, when they suffer, so do you. In the most profound sense, whatever the nature of your sufferings, Jesus suffers with and for you because you are inseparably united to him.

As We Suffer with Christ, We *Fill Up* His Sufferings

This is a great mystery. Paul exclaims, *I rejoice in my sufferings… I am filling up what is lacking in Christ's afflictions* (Colossians 1:24).

Jesus identifies with our sufferings and owns them as His. He co-suffers with his people. Interrogating Paul for his murderous persecution of the church, Jesus asks him, *Why do you persecute me?* Anyone who persecutes a Christian persecutes Jesus.

All our acts are connected to Jesus. He commends or condemns our deeds as something done to him.

> *In that you did this to one of the least of these you also did it to me… In that you did not do it to the least of these, you did not do it to me.* (Matthew 25:40,45)

The Chief Purpose of Our Sufferings

Enduring trials works growth in love, joy and righteousness.

> *Count it all joy my brothers when you meet trials of various kinds. For you know that the testing of your faith produces steadfastness. And let steadfastness have its full effect, that you may be perfect <teleion> and complete, lacking in nothing.* (James 1:3,4)

There is an even higher purpose to our sufferings. No matter what temporal or spiritual blessings result, the Spirit's chief purpose for your spiritual battles is that you might own and experience the fellowship of Christ's sufferings.

> *Because of the surpassing worth of knowing Christ Jesus my Lord.* **For his sake I have suffered the loss of all things and count them as rubbish** *in order that I might gain Christ…*

that I might know him and the power of his resurrection, **and may share (Koinonia) in his sufferings, becoming like him in his death,** *that by any means I may attain the resurrection of the dead.* (Philippians 3:10)

The finish line of the Christian life, and the supreme purpose of our trials is the fellowship of Christ's sufferings. That we may share in his sufferings, becoming like him in his death so we might be raised. This explains why the church, throughout its long history, has regarded martyrdom—dying for Jesus—as the greatest honor any believer can experience.

What a consolation and comfort in all our warfare! Nothing compares with the unspeakable honor and privilege of knowing that we are Jesus' friends and are filling up His sufferings.

TESTIMONY

The Groan of Christ for a City

Our Expedition Against the Darkness in North Africa

I recall two graphic experiences of experiencing Christ's suffering while travelling to North Africa with leaders of World Harvest Mission.

The first night, we stayed in a hotel at the center of the capital city. I woke up at about 6 a.m. with repeated megaphonic cries blaring from the top of a Muslim minaret right next to my room at the hotel. The crier roused us; "Wake up and pray! Wake up and pray! It is better to pray than to sleep. Wake and pray!"

Fully wakened, I follow his exhortation. I begin to pray. I turn to the place I was reading from in my Trinity hymnal and read these encouraging words:

> Be lifted up your heads, you gates of brass;
> Ye bars of iron yield;
> And let the king of glory pass;
> The cross is in the field.
> A holy war his servants wage;
> in that mysterious strife,
> The powers of heaven and hell engage;
> more than death or life.
>
> —James Montgomery, "Lift Up Your Heads, Ye Gates of Brass"

I realized that long before our arrival, a battle of kingdoms had already been raging. I was entering into Christ's suffering and care for this lost people.

A few days later, we visited a city of a million people—entirely Muslim, with only a handful of well concealed Christians. For safety, believers live undercover. We explored the possibility of sending a mission team to set up a mission post at a local art college. The goal was to build a bridge through meaningful conversations mediated by the arts. Driving through the town, I was struck with the colorful clothing of the women and the many attractive young people walking the streets.

Later that day we piled into our cars and drove away from the city. Reaching the outskirts, I distinctly heard a repeated and deep cry of sorrow, almost a wailing, rising from the city behind us.

This was not audible, yet the cry was as clear and palpable as if spoken aloud. I understood in these sounds of sorrow, the soul of this benighted people was crying out, "Why are you leaving us? Won't you come back? Deliver us from our sorrow, from our ignorance of Christ, from our captivity to the Dark Enemy. We beg of you, come back! Bring others with you!"

Could it be that I was hearing the Spirit of Christ, *groaning with unutterable groanings* with the soul of that city and on behalf of those million souls whom he had created, cared for and suffered long over?

Though God's people be scarce or absent, every human being and people group is under the immediate care of God and the object of his saving desire, *who desires all men to be saved* (1 Timothy 2:4). God plants, care for, grieves over, and desires the salvation of every city and every soul within:

> *You pitied the plant, for which you did not labor, nor did you make it grow, which came into being in a night and perished in a night. And should I not pity Nineveh, that great city, in which there are more than 120,000 persons who do not know their right hand from their left?* (Jonah 4:10,11)

God taught Jonah that he was not the first evangelist to Nineveh. God did not arrive at the same time Jonah did. His Spirit was there all along—nurturing its life, quickening its conscience, grieving its cruel sins. True to God's word, even when sent by man, every time an evangelist missionary, campus worker, or church planter enters a needy field of unbelievers, he is ultimately responding to the cry and call of Christ who has been in their midst from the beginning.

PART III

Engage for Conquest

*Therefore take up the whole armor of God,
that you may be able to withstand in the evil day.*

(Ephesians 6:13)

In Section I we identified the main antagonists in spiritual warfare. In Section II we have discerned their strategy. We will not be outwitted by Satan for *we are not ignorant of his designs* (2 Corinthians 2:11). The next question is, "What are we to do about the advancing phalanx of evil?"

There is good news. We can engage and overcome the enemy. Christ has given us a strategy. We have an arsenal of spiritual weapons that tear down enemy strongholds. The Scriptures teach that Kingdom prayer allied with bold evangelism is the heavy artillery.

In the first chapter of this section, we will study how public evangelism is as important as pulpit preaching. We go on to add that prayer ignites, sustains, and completes the missionary task. John Bunyan said it well:

> You can do more than pray after you have prayed,
> but you cannot do more than pray until you have prayed.
> Pray often, for prayer is a shield to the soul, a sacrifice to God,
> and a scourge to Satan.

Yet not just any prayer will do! To effectively engage evil, we must ask God to restrain evildoers and overthrow their plans. We apply ourselves to the challenging task of praying military prayers. This is the burden of Chapters 13 and 14.

In chapter 15, we conclude our study on a triumphant note. In the New Testament narrative, we discover abundant evidence that withstanding of the enemy opens the door to miraculous fruitfulness.

CHAPTER 12

We Have First Strike Capability

> "Some wish to live within the sound of church
> and chapel bell. I want to run a rescue shop
> within a yard of hell."
>
> —C.T. Studd

> "If I had my choice, I wouldn't send you to school,
> I'd send you to hell for five minutes
> and you'd come back real soul winners."
>
> —William Booth

> *I will build my church and the gates of hell*
> *shall not prevail against it.*
>
> (Matthew 16:18)

In armed conflict the army that initiates the first strike is often the victor. Cripple the airfields, destroy the fortifications, target the armories and you have already won half the battle.

We need not wait until we are under siege and the enemy is entrenched before a call to arms. We have first strike capability and abundant weaponry to destroy strongholds (2 Corinthians 10:4).

Jesus did not come to bring peace, but a sword (Matthew 10:34-36). The gospel message is a declaration of war against the enemy of our souls. United prayer and bold public evangelism constitute an incursion into enemy territory. Sustained prayer and gospel proclamation render the enemy defenseless.

> *When a strong man, fully armed, guards his own palace, his goods are safe; but when one stronger than he attacks him and overcomes him, he takes away his armor in which he trusted and divides his spoil.* (Luke 11:21,22)

Preaching on the Streets

Spiritual warfare centers on public proclamation of the gospel. As the apostles demonstrate time and again, witnessing about Jesus is on the streets, in the marketplace, and from house to house. There are a variety of Greek words used to denote this kind of street level proclamation. Paul's farewell discourse to the Ephesian elders unpacks several.

> *You know that I have not hesitated to **preach** anything that would be helpful to you but have **taught you publicly** and from house to house. I have **declared** to both Jews and Greeks that they must turn to God in repentance and have faith in our Lord Jesus… my only aim is to finish the race and complete the task the Lord Jesus has given me—the task of **testifying to the good news** of God's grace. … I have gone about **preaching the kingdom** …* (Acts 20:17-25)

We tend to think of "preaching" as a pastor delivering a sermon on Sunday morning. However, the purpose of apostolic preaching reaches beyond teaching the flock. Paul uses several words to express the "out there" nature of proclamation.

Preach, *agello*, means to announce a message publicly. *I have not hesitated to preach anything that would be helpful to you.* **Teaching**, *didaskalo*, was not confined to the assembly, *I have taught you publicly and from house to house.* To **declare**, *martureo*, from which we get martyr, means to bear witness publicly—as in a court of law; *I have **declared** to both Jews and Greeks that*

they must turn to God in repentance and have faith in our Lord Jesus.
Testify to the good news is literally to evangelize, *euangelizdo*.
Preaching the kingdom is *kerusso*, meaning to herald abroad, announcing victory into the highways, byways, and centers of a conquered realm.

Recovering spiritual warfare and restoring gospel proclamation to its full power and purpose happens when ministers of the gospel step out of the safe confines of church gatherings and bring the message of the Kingdom into their community.

Bold Evangelism Yields Abundant Harvest

Peter's sermon at the beginning of Acts provides an example of the kind of uncompromising preaching that saves souls:

> *Let all the house of Israel therefore know for certain that God has made him both Lord and Christ, this Jesus whom you crucified." Now when they heard this they were cut to the heart, and said to Peter and the rest of the apostles, "Brothers, what shall we do?" And Peter said to them, "Repent and be baptized every one of you in the name of Jesus Christ for the forgiveness of your sins, and you will receive the gift of the Holy Spirit." ... So those who received his word were baptized, and there were added that day about three thousand souls.* (Acts 2:36-38, 41)

The effect of bold evangelism is the promised harvest. The New Testament narrative is not shy about numbers. The early Church measured the Spirit's advance in the language of arithmetic, *arithmos*. Luke also uses the word for "multiply," *plethuno*, several times (i.e., 6:7, 12:24, 13:49, 19:20); the word expresses the gospel message is the seed that bears a hundred-fold.

Luke tells us that the **number** of men came to be about five thousand (Acts 4:4); the **number** of the disciples **multiplied greatly** in Jerusalem, and **a great many priests** became obedient to the faith (Acts 6:7); in the comfort of the Holy Spirit, the church **multiplied**...(Acts 9:31); and **a great many** people were added to the Lord (Acts 11:24).

History proves that when leaders are bold to evangelize, their obedience is contagious. It is like when thousands of wildebeest gather at the banks of the crocodile-infested Mara River. Even though green pastures beckon on the far side, the animals cower in fear and crowd on shore until their boldest leaders take the plunge—after that, the masses follow. Yes, a few are devoured, but thousands are saved.

The same principle applies to the Church. Believers follow their leaders when they evangelize. We read that *they were all filled with the Holy Spirit and continued to speak the word of God with boldness* (Acts 4:31).

Christians desire to share their faith. They love their unsaved friends but are held back by fear. Compromisers counsel Christians to stay put and stay safe, warning "You might offend someone." A timid flock waits for a few bold leaders to plunge into the rivers of gospel conversation; once they dive in, members follow. Yes, they are persecuted for the cause, but this only drives them to their knees, pleading for more power. Only the compromisers end up disappointed.

There is more good news. Following the pouring out of the Holy Spirit in Acts, not only are there thousands of conversions, but there are also many mighty acts of deliverance and a torrent of spectacular healings.

Let us not tone down the cosmic significance of Christ's saving work. Pray eagerly and expectantly for healings, deliverance, special guidance, and other wonderful works of God. When our prayers are fueled by faith and guided by God's promises, we can be confident that God will speak and act with power.

Waiting in Prayer Is Both Preparation and Engagement

Courageous evangelism that results in a river of conversions flows from the headwaters of the resurrection and enthronement of Christ.

> *Wait for the gift my Father promised, which you have heard me speak about. For John baptized with water, but in a few days you will be baptized with the Holy Spirit.* (Acts 1:4-5 NIV)

Waiting is obedience translated into prayer. The disciples had seen the risen Christ. They were eager and willing to head out, yet they had to wait in prayer before proceeding. The battle they would face was hard-pitched and to-the-death, with every advance met by counterattack. So, they waited in prayer: *All these with one accord were devoting themselves to prayer, together with the women and Mary the mother of Jesus…*(Acts 1:14).

"Wait" is a profound and pregnant word in Scripture and in a Christian's life.

Therefore, the LORD waits to be gracious to you,
and therefore he exalts himself to show mercy to you …
blessed are all those who wait for him. (Isaiah 30:18)

From of old no one has heard or perceived by the ear,
no eye has seen a God besides you, who acts for those
who wait for him. (Isaiah 64:4)

When the Lord tells his followers to wait, it is a cease-and-desist order: "Whatever you are doing … stop!" Jesus warns that we dare not move ahead without calibrating our plans with him, as *apart from me you can do nothing* (John 15:5). If you go ahead without waiting, you go ahead alone.

Waiting is not a cessation of activity! Waiting is filled with prayer. To wait on God is to pray; to pray is to wait on God.

Jesus' command to wait is overwhelmed by the greatness of his promise. Waiting is pregnant with expectation; *Wait for the promise, you will receive power when the Holy Spirit comes upon you and you will be my witnesses … to the end of the earth* (Acts 1:4,8). Waiting on God expectantly anticipates the supernatural presence and power of Christ.

Waiting on God reverses the ratio of joy in relation to expectation. The numbers are an educated guess but we call it the 80/20 principle. Go ahead in your own plans and 80 percent of your life will be predictable and 20 percent unexpected. Wait on Jesus in prayer and 20 percent of your life will be predictable, and 80 percent will be infused with the surprising work of the Holy Spirit.

HOW TO PRAY

A Prayer for Gospel Ministers to Engage

"Through days of preparation, thy grace has made us strong." The stirring battle hymn "Lead On, O King Eternal" inspires us to be ready, equipped, and engaged in fields of conquest and to endure the conflict that inevitably follows. Lord, you have commissioned us with your authority; you have promised to empower us by your Spirit. Your gospel is the power of God unto salvation. Help us to take you at your word and promise—you will build your church, and the gates of hell shall not prevail.

We confess that we have devoted untold hours and spent vast sums of money in our seminaries and churches for battle preparation, but too often have been reluctant to follow our Lord into the fray. We repent, we are commanded by Christ and the archangels to go forth into the world and preach the gospel to every creature (Revelation 14:6), yet we have often confined this gospel to gatherings of believers.

We lament before you Lord that we seldom experience the more joy in heaven of the one sinner who repents (Luke 15:7). We boldly announce that we are not ashamed of the gospel, but our silence betrays our fears. We have seldom experienced that the good news is the power of God unto salvation—not because we have tried and failed, but because we have failed to try.

We start new churches with good intentions but design our ministries and services to attract Christians or corral those who are unhappy in other churches.

We repent heartily that we have buried our talents and treasures in the ground.

Forgive us Lord. Give us a Holy Spirit resolve to turn from this terrible sin of omission, to make Christ known to unbelievers, and to endure the hostility that he endured while he dwelt among us. Amen.

TESTIMONY

Victory Without Vigilance Is Short-Lived
Stories from Church Planters

For seven years, I served as home missions director for our denomination. I recall the tragic testimonies of unprepared church planters brought down by enemy attack.

A mission in the Midwest started like gangbusters. It grew to 160 attenders in just two years, including many newcomers to the faith and several conversions. By the end of the second year, the church divided, and the founding pastor resigned, exhausted and disillusioned. When I asked what happened, he sadly said, "Satan attacked us from all sides, in the church and me personally. I had grown spiritually lazy. I just wasn't prepared."

A mission pastor in the western Rockies suffered a similar fate. Attendance quickly shot up to 200, with many new to the faith. One evening, a woman who had recently converted came to visit the mission pastor's wife. He explained that his wife was out of town—but invited her in anyway. He mixed a pitcher of margaritas. You can guess what happened next. He called me the next morning to confess. Thankfully this brother humbled himself, reconciled with his wife and was restored to fellowship immediately, and to pastoral ministry years later.

A third example is a seasoned mission pastor on the west coast who had been an effective evangelist in previous church plants. The city he chose to plant in was hostile territory. He struggled for a few years, but the project failed, and he fell into immorality. When asked by a friend what went wrong, his reply was simple: "I stopped praying." It made me want to cry.

There is no shortcut to effective ministry. The minister of the gospel must be filled with the Spirit and walk with integrity.

Set the believers an example in speech, in conduct, in love, in faith, in purity ... Practice these things, immerse yourself in them .... Keep a close watch on yourself and on the teaching. Persist in this, for by so doing you will save both yourself and your hearers. (1 Timothy 4:12, 15-16)

CHAPTER 13

Learn Military Prayer in This Age of Grace

"I fear the prayers of John Knox more than an army of ten thousand men."

—Mary, Queen of Scots

"Judge eternal, throned in splendor,
the Lord of lords and King of kings,
With thy living fire of judgement,
purge this land of bitter things.
Solace all its wide dominion,
with the healing of thy wings."

—Henry Scott Holland, *Trinity Hymnal* #620

I did not come to judge the world but to save the world.

(John 12:47)

The Lord is not slow to fulfill his promise as some count slowness, but is patient toward you, not wishing that any should perish, but that all should reach repentance.

(2 Peter 3:9)

God suffers long with those who deserve judgment. When God sent Noah to build the ark, it took several decades to build. During the entire time God called Noah to be *a herald of righteousness* (2 Peter 2:5). In response to Abraham's pleading, God said he would spare a wicked city, should even ten righteous men be found in her (Genesis 18:22-33). God appointed Moses to stand in the gap between the rebellious Israelites and his wrath (Exodus 33:9-14, Numbers 14:11-19).

God commands us to pray for all people to flourish and be saved—no matter how far they have fallen into sin:

I urge, then, first of all, that petitions, prayers, intercession, and thanksgiving be made for all people—for kings and all those in authority, that we may live peaceful and quiet lives in all godliness and holiness. This is good, and pleases God our Savior, who wants all people to be saved and to come to a knowledge of the truth. For there is one God and on mediator between God and mankind, the man Christ Jesus. (1Timothy 2:1-5 NIV)

Because we are in the day of grace, no matter how dark things get or how intense our trials, we pray for our enemies and persecutors:

Love your enemies and pray for those who persecute you, so that you may be sons of your Father in heaven …You therefore must be perfect, as your heavenly father is perfect. (Matthew 5:44, 48)

We wait patiently and prayerfully for God's final vindication of his people. In the meantime, we rejoice that we live in an era of unprecedented gospel conquest. We take joy in the sound research that finds astonishing numbers are being saved. Recent data reveals that for the first time, Africa is now home to the greatest number of Christians in the world, a title previously held by Latin America. An infographic provided by the Center for the Study of Global Christianity at Gordon Conwell Theological Seminary shows that more than 631 million Christians currently reside in Africa, and they make up 45 percent of the population.[23] Since 1950, research by Equipping Leaders International estimates that the number of

---

[23] *Christian Post World,* July 11, 2018.

churches in India has grown from 100,000 to 700,000. According to a 2021 Pew Center for Research study, a significant number of Christian "untouchables" do not figure in the official count.

In 1950, there were an estimated 1 million believers in China. The number now exceeds 70 million.[24] In the Muslim world, hundreds of thousands, even millions, are opening their hearts to the gospel in ways never dreamed of.[25]

Whenever I am tempted to cry down judgment, God asks me, "John, do you really want this day of grace to end? I have taken care of your eternity. Think of those held captive by Satan and lost in sin and misery. Think of your loved ones who do not know me." As Charles Spurgeon argued, "If sinners be damned, at least let them leap to Hell over our dead bodies. And if they perish, let them perish with our arms wrapped about their knees."

When overwhelmed with evil, we can be tempted to pray for the end to come; however, these impatient prayers will be rebuffed by Jesus: *"Lord, do you want us to tell fire to come down from heaven and consume them?" But [Jesus] turned and rebuked them* (Luke 9:54-55). Prayers for vengeance will not be heard. God will execute his judgments on the day He has chosen.

While We Must Not Call Down Curses on Our Enemies, We Must Pray Against their Evil Plots and Deeds

In our own strength, we are defenseless against a superior foe. From the eighth to eleventh centuries, Vikings pillaged and plundered at will through coastal monasteries and villages, of Northern Europe and beyond. Inhabitants were totally unprepared. Relentless and ruthless, they were unstoppable. Cultivating a fierce culture of war, the Vikings glorified battle. Their terrified victims—monks, nuns, feudal lords, and peasant farmers—fled or surrendered without a fight.

---

[24] See an excellent study by a British diplomat to China, Tony Lambert, *China's Christian Millions* (Oxford: Monarch Books, 2006)., *China's Christian Millions*
[25] See David Garrison, *A Wind in the House of Islam* (Monument, CO: Wigtake Resources, 2014).

This is a fitting illustration of the world today. Asserting global dominance, the seen and unseen powers of this present age advance relentlessly—storming our spiritual, moral, and psychic gates and plundering at will. The walls of the city are crumbling.

Churches are ill-equipped to engage the well-armed, and united alliance of seen and unseen forces. Once a week Christianity is scarcely an obstacle. Some are already fleeing the field and others are surrendering. Consider recent data on the church in Canada. From 2011 to 2021, even occasional church attendance declined 17 percent, from 6 percent to 5 percent of the total population. Those who nominally affiliated as Christians have declined 11 percent, from 64 to 53 percent. Young people, ages 25 to 34, represent the greatest defection, from 57 to 37 percent.

Should we simply abandon the field and head to the hills? Not at all! Jesus has disarmed and conquered at the cross and has ascended to the highest place of authority and power. By faith we participate in the conquest of Christ: *You have been filled in him, who is the head of all rule and authority* (Colossians 2:10). We take up arms when we call upon Christ; we muster the troops and engage the enemy forces head on when we gather to pray.

We have an endless supply of Scripture promises to inspire and inform our prayers. The most quoted Psalms in the New Testament, Psalm 2 and 110, are Messianic conquest prayers. This triumph of Christ applies directly to every faithful soldier who follows Christ into battle.

> To the one who is victorious and does my will to the end, *I will give authority over the nations—that one "will rule them with an iron scepter and will dash them to pieces like pottery"—just as I have received authority from my Father. I will also give that one the morning star.* (Revelation 2:26-28 NIV, quoting Psalm 2)

We ignite the foundries, bellow the flames, and refill the armory with repentant and humble prayer.

> *If my people who are called by my name humble themselves, and pray and seek my face and turn from their wicked ways, then I will hear from heaven and will forgive their sin and heal their land.* (2 Chronicles 7:14)

When Christ's church prays, she experiences resurrection empowerment and boldness. The Holy Spirit falls, and with astonishing rapidity the Kingdom advances in the fear of God and in the face of persecution. Once revival takes root, it spreads and brings hope and renewal into the surrounding land. The leaven starts small and takes time, but eventually it changes everything.

In 1727, the church in Herrnhut, Germany, labored under a dark cloud of division. Persecuted Christians from all over the land took refuge and were received into the Moravian community. However, before long, Lutherans, Calvinists and Moravians were embroiled in bitter divisions. A tearful and repentant revival ignited in the summer of 1727. After praying all night, the entire community was overwhelmed with a realization of the sufferings of Christ. The prince of the town, Nicholas Von Zinzendorf testified, "O head full of bruises. So full of pain and scorn."

He reports, "A spirit of prayer was immediately evident in the fellowship and continued through that golden summer of 1727." Everyone, including the children, gathered in circles to pray. Zinzendorf adds, "On August 27, twenty-four men and twenty-four women covenanted to spend one hour each day in scheduled prayer." This prayer meeting lasted *100 years*—and was called The Lord's Watch. Even today, global 24/7 concerts of prayer trace their initiative to the Moravian prayer movement.[26] In the first year they send 3 couples and 8 single men to Labrador. Within 30 years, the church had sent out hundreds of missionaries.

The Day of Grace Will Not Last Forever

There comes a time when God's longsuffering comes to an end. The verdict against the evil one and his allies has already been declared, the sentence pronounced, and the day of execution set. Midnight approaches for every empire and nation that despises God and dismisses his commandments. There comes a time when a people become so steeped in wickedness, they reach the point of no return. Consider these sobering passages:

---

[26] Leslie K. Tarr, "A Prayer Meeting That Lasted 100 Years," Christian History, no. 1 (1982)

> *But they kept mocking the messengers of God, despising his words and scoffing at his prophets, until the wrath of the LORD rose against his people, until there was no remedy.* (2 Chronicles 36:16)

> *There is no faithfulness, no love, no acknowledgment of God in the land. There is only cursing, lying and murder, stealing and adultery; they break all bounds, and bloodshed follows bloodshed. Because of this the land dries up, and all who live in it waste away … The more priests there were, the more they sinned against me… I will punish them for their ways and repay them for their deeds.* (Hosea 4:1-9 NIV)

> *Because lawlessness will be increased, the love of many will grow cold.* (Matthew 24:12)

> *Night is coming, when no one can work.* (John 9:4)

In every age, God declares to tyrants that their time is up:

> *God has numbered the days of your kingdom and brought it to an end. You have been weighed in the balances and found wanting.* (Daniel 5:26-27)

Nineveh was spared in Jonah's time, but ultimately met her doom. Her reprieve was temporary. A century later, the prophet Nahum prophesies Nineveh's end:

> *The LORD is a jealous and avenging God; the LORD is avenging and wrathful; the LORD takes vengeance on his adversaries and keeps wrath for his enemies. The LORD is slow to anger and great in power, and the LORD will by no means clear the guilty.* (Nahum 1:2-3)

God declares that he is both a longsuffering Savior and unyielding judge of those who despise him:

> *You shall not bow down to them or worship them; for I, the LORD your God, am a jealous God, punishing the children for the sin of the parents to the third and fourth generation of those who hate me, but showing love to a thousand generations of those who love me and keep my commandments.* (Deuteronomy 5:9-10 NIV)

These warnings are not theoretical. Prayerfully and honestly, we can look at our own nation and ask, "Are our days numbered as well?" Every form of godlessness, adultery, cursing of God and man, hardness of heart, and lawlessness have accumulated for generations, with no repentance or desire to repent. How many of our leaders and rulers in government, judiciary, professional fields, and industry have been weighed in the balance and found wanting?

It is time for us to pray for our nation, "Lord, we lay crushed and dehumanized under the weight and burden of our sin. Our lawlessness, greed, envy, and avarice testify against us. Our individual and national conscience has been silenced. Our transgressions are heaped up to heaven. Pour out your spirit of prayer so we can weep unconsolably and seek you for mercy."

Until the clock strikes midnight, a governor has power to grant a stay of execution. Because we live in the age of grace, an offer of clemency stands up to last hour. If we repent, God will postpone judgement. It was true for wicked Nineveh, when Jonah declared, *Yet forty days, and Nineveh shall be overthrown!* (Jonah 3:4) It was true in King Josiah's day: *Because your heart was penitent … your eyes shall not see all the disaster I will bring upon this place* (2 Kings 22:19-20). It was also true in Hosea's day:

> *Come let us return to the LORD;*
> *for he has torn us, that he may heal us;*
> *he has struck us down, and he will bind us up.*
> *After two days he will revive us;*
> *on the third day he will raise us up,*
> *that we may live before him.*
> *Let us know; let us press on to know the LORD.*
> (Hosea 6:1-3)

May it be true in ours.

A Military Prayer

Who consider the power of your anger, and your wrath according to the fear of you (Psalm 90:11). We confess that we have provoked you to anger and that our sins have mounted to the very courts of heaven.

You are just and holy, we are rebellious and sinful. We are judged and soon to be judged. Teach us godly anger—to own our sin, hate it, and repent in tears, and holy resolve to turn from our destructive ways. If we repent, may it be in your infinite mercy and because of the blood sacrifice of your Son for sinners that you will relent concerning your righteous judgments and our certain doom.

How To Pray Military Prayers

When we ask God to defend us, we can direct our prayers to Jesus. He is the Redeemer and the judge of humankind. *The Father judges no one but has given all judgment to the Son* (John 5:22). This very day, Jesus rules the nations with a rod of iron (Psalm 2:9). He rules *in midst of his enemies* (Psalm 110:2).

In the final day, *the day of Christ* (Philippians 1:6), Jesus will judge the whole world.

Behold the Lord comes with ten thousand of his holy ones, to execute judgment on all the people of the world. He will convict every person of all the ungodly things they have done and for all the insults that ungodly sinners have spoken against him. (Jude 14-15)

We can be confident that God will hear and answer our prayers to restrain and overthrow evil. The reason Jesus came was to *destroy the works of the devil* (1 John 3:8), therefore we pray: "Lord Jesus, we ask that you destroy the works of the devil and frustrate and overthrow the plans and activities of all those who do the works of the devil."

There are Biblical passages we can pray when asking God to act against the wicked. Consider this Psalm.

Lord, confuse the wicked, confound their words, for I see violence and strife in the city. Day and night they prowl about on its walls; malice and abuse are within it. Destructive forces are at work in the city; threats and lies never leave its streets.

As for me, I call to God, and the LORD saves me …
He rescues me unharmed from the battle waged against me …
God, who is enthroned from of old, who does not change—
he will hear them and humble them, because they have no fear of God.

(Psalm 55:9-11,16-19)

The Scriptures tell us that *God* will destroy *the destroyers of the earth* (Revelation 11:18). Leaving the time and manner of judgment to God, this verdict can inform our prayers against evil. We can pray; "Creator of all the earth, we know that you will judge those who ravage the earth and its inhabitants. Act speedily we pray, for we languish under this oppression."

We must pray against the laws, schemes, and lies of those who would frustrate the advance of the gospel. When heresy threatens, we pray against the false prophets. *If anyone destroys God's temple, God will destroy him; for God's temple is holy, and you are that temple.* (1 Corinthians 3:17). Praying against opposition to the gospel of Christ is mandated for believers.

"Great Shepherd, we are attacked from without by savage wolves and ravaged from within by wolves in sheep's clothing. Defend us, Lord! In your day, destroy those who would destroy your Church. We ask that you grant conversion to our opponents, banish the wolves from your flock. In this hour of trial, we pray for you to overthrow and confound the worldly powers who repress the gospel proclamation. Amen"

TESTIMONY

Prayer in the Halls of a High School
A Student's Military Prayer

At the end of the annual Christmas program at the church we attend, a high school senior named Alia shared her testimony about the spiritual challenges in her local school and then led us in prayer. Here is her testimony and prayer:

"This year, a friend and I formed a prayer group at school with our other Christian friends. Five of us meet during lunch once a week with the purpose of supporting each other in our faith and praying against the darkness in our school.

School can be a wonderful place of community and learning, but it can also be a dark place. On the first day of the week, you go home, and you feel tired, but by the end of the week you feel a deeper sense of exhaustion. This is not normal exhaustion—it is spiritual exhaustion. There's a battle going on in our school and it needs prayer! My peers (especially girls) often look for their identity in dark places, leading to depression, anxiety, and even self-hatred. Alcohol and drug abuse are common. It's a frequent occurrence to go into a bathroom and find kids vaping. Addiction is prevalent, not only to substances but to things like social media.

Inspired by this testimony, as a congregation, we formed groups and prayed the following requests:

- That the grace of Christ would fill the atmosphere of the school.
- For Christ to work mightily against depression, anxiety, and self-hatred.
- To intercede for those teenagers turning to drugs and addiction.

Following a time of congregational prayer for the young people in our community, this high school prayer warrior concluded by praying:

"Dear Heavenly Father,

I want to lift up our schools to you today, the schools in our province, our district, elementary, middle, high school, universities, colleges, all of them. But I especially want to lift up George Elliot High School to you today. Free my school from bondage. I pray that this cycle of evil would be broken. I ask that your presence would fill this place and reach into every corner, bringing rejuvenation. In the name of Jesus Christ, I cast out the spirits of depression, anxiety, and addiction that have been allowed to take hold. There is power in Your Name and we decree it over George Elliot today. I ask that your truth would reign over all the lies. That this veil would be removed so that others would see the battle we are fighting and answer the call to take up their cross and join.

I pray that you would give courage to those of us who are already fighting. I ask that you teach us how to put on our armor and protect us from the enemy's attacks. I pray that we would have a burning desire to live for you, a desire that would shine through everything we do and be contagious to everyone around us, so that when they walk into George Elliot, instead of feeling this crushing sense of despair they would experience your love. Jesus, we declare that you reign over George Elliot.

We thank you for who you are and for hearing our prayers. We ask all this in your name. Amen."

CHAPTER 14

Cultivate Holy Anger Against an Unholy Enemy

> "Demonize demons. Humanize humans."
>
> —Salvation Army Director

> "Lord, keep us steadfast in your word;
> curb those who by craft and sword,
> *Would wrest the Kingdom from thy Son,*
> and bring to naught all he has done."
>
> —Martin Luther

In the previous chapter we argued, though we live in the age of grace, praying against evil is an essential dimension of spiritual warfare. While we forgive and pray for our enemies and bless those who persecute us, we also pray boldly against those who plot to oppress the innocent and seek to destroy the witness of Christ. Often neglected in our time, perhaps nothing is more important than praying, *Deliver us from evil*.

Courageous, Bold Prayer Is the Christian's Means for Engaging Enemies Within and Without

In graphic language, John Fletcher tackles a challenging passage which explains the warfare nature of prayer: *The kingdom of heaven suffers violence, and the violent take it by force* (Matthew 11:12).

The kingdom permits certain kinds of violence. One kind is toward those lords who reign over us—the world, the flesh, and the devil. These rebels must be turned out. Our own wills must be overcome, and ourselves surrendered up to God… Further, a humble, holy, sacred violence must be used in prayer; with Jesus—that he would open in our hearts the power of faith, apply the efficacy of his blood, and bestow on us a spirit of prayer, in other words the prayer of faith… that he would look through the pillar of fire and discomfit our enemies and with the Holy Spirit that he would look through the pillar of fire and take up his abode with us…The words allude to the taking of a fortified ton by storming it. This is of all military expeditions the most dangerous. The enemy is covered and hidden, and those who scale the walls have nothing but their arms and courage… The prayer of repentance, the prayer of faith, storm mount Sion, the city of God. He that is violent shall receive the kingdom of God… But remember, the violent bear it away by force. There shall be many hard struggles with God's enemies… before He declares us conqueror.

—John Fletcher, Meditations

Saints of old categorized prayer as precatory, deprecatory, and imprecatory. Each of these kinds of prayer is needed for effective spiritual warfare.

Precatory prayer is asking for good things from God through Christ, such as a fresh filling of the Holy Spirit, transformed motives, the fruits of a renewed life, courage to take a stand against evil, and the power to boldly defend the truth.

Deprecatory prayer is when we pray against the inner accusations and attacks of Satan. Bryan Zacharias describes it this way:

> It is to be used in midst of suffering as another instance of warfare praying, since Satan often attacks saints who are undergoing affliction: Deprecate the snare and temptation that suffering may expose you to.[27]

---

[27] Bryan Zacharias, *The Embattled Christian* (Chicago: Moody Publishers, 2018), 109.

Imprecatory prayer is asking God to destroy the works of the devil and to confound the wicked in their schemes against God and the Church. It is asking for God, in his time, to vindicate his name and take vengeance on those who hate him and oppose his Kingdom.

We are not helpless *against this present darkness* (Ephesians 6:12). When we consecrate our days to intercessory prayer, we do our part to restrain the tide of wickedness threatening to overwhelm Church and nation. God will hear our prayers, forgive our sins, and heal our land (2 Chronicles 7:14). He will answer our plea and rescue us from *this present evil age* (Galatians 1:4).

However, praying effectively against God's enemies requires spiritual maturity. We must pray boldly and confidently against evil. Yet as we pray, there should be no hint of malice or vengefulness. Like God, we take no joy in the punishment of the wicked. Even as we pray against evil laws and decrees, we continue to pray for our rulers.

> *Do not rejoice when your enemy falls and let not your heart be glad when he stumbles, lest the LORD see it and be displeased, and turn away his anger from him. Fret not yourself because of evildoers, and be not envious of the wicked ... My son, fear the LORD and the king, and do not join with those who do otherwise.* (Proverbs 24:17-21)

We can and must pray against Satan and his allies. We pray for the honor of God and the defense of the vulnerable. Our prayers are not directed against personal enemies. Tim Keller points out that we must always take care that there is no personal rancor behind our anger against evildoers: "Everything in the Bible tells the Christian that we must never desire the harm of the person who offended us—never!"[28]

When motives are purified by the Spirit, we can pray for Christ to destroy the work of Satan. *The reason the Son of God appeared was to destroy the works of the devil* (1 John 3:8). Committing the timing to God, we can pray that he would confound, restrain, and rout those who seek to murder, deface, or destroy image bearers of God.

---

[28] Tim Keller, *Forgive*, 195

God will destroy *the destroyers of the earth* (Revelation 11:18). When heretics or persecutors seek to destroy the Church, we can pray boldly against their wicked schemes: *If anyone destroys God's temple, God will destroy him … You are God's temple* (1 Corinthians 3:17).

The following hymn is a prayer for God to restrain, remove, or convert the enemies of the Church, asking God to vindicate his people and judge his enemies, or, best of all, grant them repentance.

> O God, no longer hold Thy peace, no longer silent be;
> Thy enemies lift up their head to fight Thy saints and Thee.
> Against Thy own, whom Thou dost love,
> their craft Thy foes employ;
> they think to cut Thy people off, Thy people would destroy.
>
> Make them like dust and stubble blown before the whirlwind dire, in terror driv'n before the storm of Thy consuming fire.
> Confound them in their sin till they to Thee for pardon fly,
> till in dismay they trembling own that Thou art GOD Most High.
>
> —Hymn Writer Anonymous

Failing to pray against evil is a form of unbelief. In a world of increasing evil, we cannot stand by and watch many millions go to hell. We must never forget that God oversees evil as well as good. We pray against evil, keeping in mind the present rule and reign of Christ over the nations and all seen and unseen powers. (Matthew 28:16; Ephesians 1:22,23).

We hear about those who silently stand and watch while a helpless victim is beaten by thugs. It is shameful to be bystanders while evildoers carry on their destructive works. Every believer can do their part. Prayer is the primary way a believer moves from being a spectator to actively engaging the enemy. It is a matter of integrity. The honor of God, the defense of the innocent, and the freedom of the Church is at stake.

Yes, there is risk involved when we defend the defenseless. The antagonist hates being interrupted in an act of violence. When wicked forces prey on Church and nation, Jesus encourages us not to fear: *In the world you will have tribulation. But take heart; I have overcome the world* (John 16:33).

Praying against evil is a team action. "The Church Militant" is a designation handed down to us from the ancient Church. This term refers to reality that all believers are united in a continual war against a common enemy. We are never more united than when we pray in one Spirit against a common foe.

God Is Longsuffering, Yet His Anger Is Righteous

Holy wrath is an attribute of a holy God. From a purified heart, we can say "Amen!" to his anger. Moses, was known to be *the meekest man alive* (Numbers 12:3). He prayed: *Who considers the power of your anger, and your wrath according to the fear of you?* (Psalm 90:11)

God's anger is just, fair, and measured. His wrath always has a perfect motive. God's attributes of love, mercy, and wrath are never in conflict. His punishment of the wicked is restorative, not reactive: *God arose to establish judgment, to save all the humble of the earth* (Psalm 76:9).

Human anger, on the other hand, is seldom just, fair, the right motive, or balanced with compassion. This world's anger is self-serving and self-justifying. The Bible is filled with warnings about unleashing anger: *Anger does not work the righteous life God requires* (James 1:20). While divine anger is restorative, devilish anger is destructive: *A man without self-control is like a city broken into and without walls* (Proverbs 25:28).

The good news is Christians can learn holy anger. Scripture encourages us to cultivate holy anger against an unholy enemy. *The fear of the LORD is hatred of evil* (Proverbs 8:13). In the language of the psalmist:

O you who love the Lord, hate evil! (Psalm 97:10)

Do I not hate those who hate you? ... Search me, O God, and know my heart! (Psalm 139:21, 23)

The Scripture cautions us to *be angry but do not sin and give no opportunity to the devil* (Ephesians 4:26-27). Holy anger comes from God. Unholy anger is from another source altogether. Longsuffering and grief accompany divine anger. Malice and vindictiveness are evidence of the devil's anger.

Jesus is the perfect amalgam of human and divine holy anger. No one images God's love, tender mercy, kindness, and justice like Jesus. No one demonstrates the perfect anger of God like Jesus. If we want to combine kindness and holy anger, we need to study Jesus.

When the Pharisees dismissed the suffering and pain of a crippled man, Jesus *looked around at them with anger, grieved at their hardness of heart* (Mark 3:5). When temple leaders barred Gentiles from worshipping God, Jesus was furious, unleashing whip and overturning tables (John 2:17). When Pharisees and priests perpetuated sham righteousness, exploited widows, and looked down on others, Jesus pronounced a sevenfold, *Woe unto you!* (Matthew 23:13-33). Jesus taught that those who harden their hearts to the poor and needy will be cast into the outer darkness (Matthew 25:41-46).

The father has committed judgement to his son (John 5:22-24). Jesus is meek. At the same time, Jesus is also mighty warrior. The forever king is the forever judge. The scriptures say it was Jesus who delivered the Israelites from Egypt; it was Jesus who destroyed those who didn't believe; it was Jesus who destroyed Sodom; it was Jesus who conquered and consigned the fallen angels to hell (Jude 1:5-7). The mercy of the lamb, and the wrath of the lamb are in perfect symmetry (Revelation 6:16,17).

Righteous anger is a gift of God whereby the justice, fairness, and right intent of God's holy anger is imparted to a believer's heart. Apart from a regenerating and sanctifying work of God, our anger always falls short.

The prophet Isaiah cried out, *"I am a man of unclean lips, and I live among the people of unclean lips."* This severe outlook indicates a deep awareness of Isaiah's own sin. We all share the ruination of mankind and it's just condemnation. Apart from the grace of God there is no hope for any of us. Only the humble and meek can uphold the righteousness of God in this generation. Failing to own our complicity makes any announcement of judgement ugly and hypocritical.

We learn holy anger in Christ's school of prayer. As we read, pray, and practice Christ's words, the Holy Spirit will impart Jesus' perfect balance of lovingkindness and righteous anger. Prayer metabolizes the word of Christ so that the character of Christ is internalized.

Vengeance Is the Lord's

The Bible teaches that God's coming judgment is as certain as Christ's second coming.

> *God is just: He will pay back trouble to those who trouble you and give relief to you who are troubled, and to us as well. This will happen when the Lord Jesus is revealed from heaven in blazing fire with his powerful angels. He will punish those who do not know God and do not obey the gospel of our Lord Jesus.* (2 Thessalonians 1:6-8 NIV)

A reckoning for evildoers is promised:

> *The wicked band together against the righteous and condemn the innocent to death. ... He will repay them for their sins and destroy them for their wickedness; the LORD our God will destroy them.* (Psalm 94:21, 23 NIV)

The certain judgment of God has an important implication for a believer. Because God alone is the judge of every human being, a Christian can leave judgement to him. *Judge not, that you be not judged* (Matthew 7:1). We do not have to waste time and energy judging others. We can concentrate all our time and energy on forgiving, serving, and praying for others, even our enemies.

If we don't tell God what to do with his wrath but allow him to send it when and where he wills, what does he do with it? In Jesus Christ God comes and takes the penalty of justice on himself ... "Vengeance is mine. I will repay." Taking the vengeance that was your due. Vengeance is his! He received it.[29]

When we commit judgment to God, we can wait patiently. When wickedness grows and persecution looms, desperate believers are tempted to turn to other powers for deliverance.

---

[29] Timothy Keller, *Forgive: Why Should I and How Can I?* (New York: Viking, 2022), 195–96.

As Jacques Ellul pointed out, turning to political solutions for spiritual problems is the "false presence of the Kingdom." God warns of disastrous consequences.

> *"Woe to the obstinate children," declares the LORD, "to those who carry out plans that are not mine, forming an alliance, but not by my Spirit, heaping sin upon sin; who go down to Egypt without consulting me."* (Isaiah 30:1-2, 15-17 NIV)

Differentiate Between Victims and Agents

When it comes to praying against the deceitful schemes of the wicked, we need to differentiate between antagonists and victims. The distinction is critical. When people are conscious allies and agents of Satan, they become "evangelists of evil." Their victims are often the most vulnerable. Unless they repent, those who lead others into sin are destined for eternal judgment.

> *But whoever causes one of these little ones who believe in me to sin, it would be better for him to have a great millstone fastened around his neck and to be drowned in the depth of the sea.* (Matthew 18:6)

In the Bible, there are several examples of innocent victims of evil. Take for example the daughter of the Syria—Phoenician widow. She was possessed by an unclean spirit. In compassion, Jesus delivers this suffering child. Satan is the enemy while the girl is the victim (Mark 7:24-29). Or consider the Philippian slave girl who is possessed by a spirit of divination (literally "a python spirit"). Through no choice of her own, she had been bought and trafficked into fortune telling. Her *owners* were the agents of evil and exorcism was her liberation (Acts 16:16-24). Then there is the child who was continually cast into the fire by a demon, who elicits only the pity of Christ (Mark 9:22). Many others oppressed by demons were brought to Jesus and the apostles for healing. *That evening they brought to him many that were oppressed by demons, and he cast out spirits with a word* (Matthew 8:16).

On the other hand, there are wicked people who are conscious opponents of God and allies of Satan. When false prophets and heretical teachers oppose God and the gospel we meet the enemy head on. We are required to pray imprecatory prayers against their teachings and activities. *If anyone is preaching to you a gospel contrary to the one you received, let him be accursed* (Galatians 1:9). We ask God to convert them—but also to restrain them, confound them, and destroy their plans.

While pastoring in Vancouver, I found out that a leader of a cult was attempting to lead a genuine seeker away from our church. We had seen it many times. It is no coincidence when a gospel inquirer encounters a messenger of the enemy. The misled seeker is the victim, and the false teacher is the enemy.

This man had a reputation for steering seekers from the truth of the gospel. I got his phone number and asked to meet with him at a local coffee shop. I listened to his views and shared mine. He thought I would be reasonable and accept our differences. After a lengthy exchange, he simply said, "I understand those are your views. They are not mine."

I replied, "I am not talking about a difference of opinion but about what God says is true." I quoted the Scripture warnings against anyone who tries to lead someone away from the Christian faith. He was silent, apparently unmoved. I paused, looked directly at him and said, "You need to leave this woman alone. If you continue to try to deceive or mislead her, you are in danger of God's judgement and the punishment of hell." He was shocked by my bluntness, but he clearly understood me.

In following days, many prayers were offered for this woman and for God to restrain or convert this false prophet. This young lady agreed not to meet with him and continued coming to the church.

Another example occurred at our men's prayer meeting. We prayed in concert against those who staged, promoted, and permitted the pagan mock portrayal of the Lord's Supper at the opening ceremonies of the Paris Olympics. "Lord we are jealous for your holy name. Grant repentance for this blasphemy. Destroy this work of the devil. In Jesus holy name we pray. Amen" God warns of swift destruction of God haters:

God is God, the faithful God, who keeps covenant and steadfast love with those who love him and keep his commandments, to a thousand generations, and repays to the face those who hate him, by destroying them. He will not be slack with the one who hates him. He will repay him to his face. (Deuteronomy 7:9,10)

We make no truce with anyone promoting occult practices but pray against them with the full force and authority of Christ. In Acts, Peter rebukes Simon the sorcerer, who was *in the gall of bitterness and in the bond of iniquity* (Acts 8:23). Paul calls Elymus the magician a *son of the devil and enemy of all righteousness, full of all deceit and villainy*, and struck him blind for opposing the gospel (Acts 13:10-11).

When wicked rulers persecute the Church, we pray against their plots. When Herod had James killed and planned to execute Peter, the church prayed boldly against Herod's schemes. Later, in his own time, God judged Herod, *he was eaten of worms and breathed his last* (Acts 12:23). God raises up and removes leaders at will.

The Litmus Test of Holy Anger Is a Jealousy for God

In a right spirit, jealousy is a form of holy anger. We pray rightly against evil when we are jealous for God. Consider the prayer of Elijah after his contest with the prophets of Baal: *I have been very jealous for the LORD, the God of hosts* (1 Kings 19:10).

An important indicator of a Christian's love for God is a holy jealousy and right-spirited anger when God's person or reputation is maligned. When someone uses Jesus' name as a curse, I ask them not to. If they ask why, I reply, "Because he is a friend."

When God is edited out from public forum and institutions, it should provoke sorrow and indignation. When unbelieving educators refer to nature, the universe, and the ecosystem, without giving thanks for the power and majesty of our Creator, jealous grief should fill our heart. God wants a multi-billion voice choir—those who impose a gag order will be judged.

When God's laws are held in contempt, those who love God take it personally. This is not a matter of apologetics and debate; it is a matter of frankly confronting those who dismiss God's Law:

Whoever says to the wicked, "You are in the right," will be cursed by peoples, abhorred by nations, but those who rebuke the wicked will have delight. (Proverbs 24:24-25)

If you are jealous for God, you will also be jealous for God's people. The Church is united to Jesus in such a profound way that to malign the Church is to malign Christ. To speak evil of the Church is to speak evil of his bride. The Church is *the fullness of him who fills all in all* (Ephesians 1:23). The grafting of the Church into his very being is why Christ gave his life: *To him be glory in the church and in Christ Jesus throughout all generations* (Ephesians 3:21). It is a popular practice of the godless to aim diatribes against the people of God, but those who love the Church never join in.

How to Intercede in Holiness

Christian intercession, motivated by a divine gift of holy anger against evil, is combined with holy concern for those ensnared by the devil. There is no prayer of Scripture that we cannot pray if we keep five things in mind:

1. **Ensure that the glory and honor of God be uppermost in our prayer.** Ask God to defend his own name against those who dishonor or hate him. Above all, leave vengeance to God, both in the timing and nature of his judgments. This leaves you free to bless and forgive our enemies.

2. **Pray for the Church, her freedom of assembly, freedom to organize, and freedom to carry out her mission for Christ—** and pray against all those who would legislate laws or policies that interfere with this holy calling. Humbly ask that God to confound, frustrate, even destroy their plans, and restrain or convert these enemies of the gospel.

3. **Pray boldly against all those who preach a false gospel** in the church or promote lies and destructive teachings in the world at large. These evangelists of evil must be confronted with bold, military prayer.

4. **Prayer against evil must be on behalf of others;** prayers must not be about defending our own person, property, or well-being. We are to turn the other cheek and forgive those who insult or attack us personally.

5. **Intercede for the vulnerable and exploited in our cities—** against trafficking; against destructive teaching of the young; and against the laws, policies, and practices of those who make life miserable for any that cannot defend themselves.

HOW TO PRAY

A Biblical Example of How Holy Prayer Routs an Unholy Enemy

2 Chronicles 20 gives us a powerful example of how Christians can pray when besieged by evil forces. King Jehoshaphat's prayer combines all the essential elements of holy anger. He is jealous for God's honor, confesses personal and national helplessness, has righteous antipathy against those who would destroy God's people, and calls on God's people to unite in prayer.

It all begins when King Jehoshaphat hears that Jerusalem is surrounded by enemy armies:

Some people came and told Jehoshaphat, "A vast army is coming against you from Edom." ... Alarmed, Jehoshaphat resolved to inquire of the LORD, and he proclaimed a fast for all Judah. The people of Judah came together to seek help from the LORD; indeed, they came from every town in Judah to seek him (20:2-4 NIV).

Jehoshaphat prays for God to vindicate his own honor.

LORD, the God of our ancestors, are you not the God who is in heaven? You rule over all the kingdoms of the nations.

Power and might are in your hand, and no one can withstand you. Our God ... [You promised] If calamity comes upon us, whether the sword of judgment, or plague or famine, we will stand in your presence before this temple that bears your Name and will cry out to you in our distress, and you will hear us and save us ... For we have no power to face this vast army that is attacking us. We do not know what to do, but our eyes are on you? (20:6-12 NIV)

Forswearing military solutions, men, women, and children unite in prayer and all Israel forms a choral army to sing praises before the Lord.

All the men of Judah, with their wives and children and little ones, stood there before the LORD. Then the Spirit of the LORD came on Jahaziel son of Zechariah ... as he stood in the assembly.

> He said: "Listen, King Jehoshaphat and all who live in Judah and Jerusalem! This is what the LORD says to you: 'Do not be afraid or discouraged because of this vast army. For the battle is not yours, but God's. ... You will not have to fight this battle. Take up your positions; stand firm and see the deliverance the LORD will give you. Do not be afraid; do not be discouraged. Go out and face them tomorrow, and the LORD will be with you.'"
>
> Consulting the people, Jehoshaphat appointed men to sing to the LORD and to praise him for the splendor of his holiness as they went out at the head of the army, saying: "Give thanks to the LORD, for his love endures forever. (20:13-17, 21 NIV)

God answers in power. The enemy is routed—confounded, divided, and self-destroyed.

> As they began to sing and praise, the LORD set ambushes against the men of Ammon and Moab and Mount Seir who were invading Judah, and they were defeated. The Ammonites and Moabites rose up against the men from Mount Seir to destroy and annihilate them. After they finished slaughtering the men from Seir, they helped to destroy one another. (20:22-23 NIV)

Afterwards, with grateful hearts King, priests and people give God the glory.

> On the fourth day they assembled... and they entered Jerusalem and went to the temple of the LORD with harps and lyres and trumpets.
>
> The fear of God came on all the surrounding kingdoms when they heard how the LORD had fought against the enemies of Israel. And the kingdom of Jehoshaphat was at peace, for his God had given him rest on every side. (20:26-30 NIV)

Preparing the Church for Persecution

A Word on Prayer as Corporate Resistance by a Contemporary Prophet

Drawing from the Old to the New Testament teachings of Jesus, Dietrich Bonhoeffer summarizes how the individual Christian and the church engage in prayer-filled spiritual warfare for our enemies.

> In persecution, our holy struggle of love and hate engage in mortal combat. It is the urgent duty of every Christian soul to prepare itself for it. The time is coming when the confession of the living God will incur not only the hatred and the fury of the world, but complete ostracism from "human society," as they call it. The Christians will be hounded from place to place, subjected to physical assault, maltreatment, and death of every kind. We are approaching the age of widespread persecution. Therein lies the true significance of all the movements and conflicts of our age.
>
> Our adversaries seek to root out the Christian Church and the Christian faith because they cannot live side by side with us, because they see in every word we utter and every deed we do, even when they are not specifically directed against them, a condemnation of their own words and deeds. They are not far wrong. They suspect too that we are indifferent to their condemnation. Indeed, they admit that it is utterly futile to condemn us. We do not reciprocate their hatred and contention, although they would like it better if we did, and so sink to their own level.
>
> And how is the battle to be fought? Soon the time will come when we shall pray, not as isolated individuals but as a corporate body, a congregation, a Church: we shall pray in multitudes (albeit in relatively small multitudes) and among the thousands and thousands of apostates we shall loudly praise and confess the Lord who was crucified and has risen and shall come again.

And what prayer, what confession, what hymn of praise will it be? It will be the prayer of earnest love for these very sons of perdition who stand around and gaze at us with eyes aflame with hatred, and who perhaps have already raised their hands to kill us. It will be a prayer for the peace of these erring, devastated and bewildered souls…

—Dietrich Bonhoeffer, *The Cost of Discipleship*,
 "The Enemy – The Extraordinary" 19

CHAPTER 15

We Are More Than Conquerors

The one who conquers and who keeps my works until the end, to him I will give authority over the nations, and he will rule them with a rod of iron, as when earthen pots are broken in pieces.

(Revelation 2:26-27)

"Lead on O king eternal, the day of march has come
Henceforth in fields of conquest, your tents have been our home.
Through days of preparation thy grace has made us strong.
And soon the night of weeping shall be the morn of song."

—Ernest Shurtleff

"The church shall never perish! Her dear Lord to defend,
to guide, sustain, and cherish, is with her to the end;
though there be those that hate her, and false sons in her pale,
against the foe or traitor she ever shall prevail."

—Samuel Stone

Kingdom advance is accompanied by loud songs of praise. The walls of Jericho were brought down with sounding trumpets and a great shout (Joshua 6:20). King Jehoshaphat's army marched to battle with a large choir in the lead. After the returning exiles overcame opposition and repaired the walls of Jerusalem,

Nehemiah appointed two great choirs to circle the city with praise, and the people joined in: *[They celebrated] the dedication with gladness, with thanksgivings and with singing, with cymbals, harps, and lyres* (Nehemiah 12:27ff).

Hymns like "Lead on O King Eternal" and "The Church's One Foundation" contain a moving summary of the essentials of spiritual warfare. Whether preparing for battles or in midst of them, loud triumphant singing wakes the soul and stirs the heart to courageous engagement like nothing else. When we join with others to sing great hymns and Scripture songs, we are roused to noble deeds. *Let the word of Christ dwell in you richly … singing psalms, hymns, and spiritual songs, with thankfulness in your heart to God* (Colossians 3:16).

Preparing to Engage

Engaging in spiritual warfare is not a matter of choice. If you're a Christian, the decision has been made. As Aragorn says to Théoden in *The Lord of the Rings*, "Open war is upon you, whether you would risk it or not." The only question is, are you prepared?

An important tactic of war is to catch the enemy unawares. Hitler marshalled the German people to build the greatest army in history—all the while convincing European leaders that he had no intent of deploying his troops. While Europe slept, German forces launched the infamous blitzkrieg, taking over whole countries in a matter of hours. It was only when Winston Churchill called the world to arms that the Nazis were stalled.

In our day, there is another kind of blitzkrieg that has caught the Church unawares. Noticed, but seldom heeded, the world has steadily grown stronger. The barbarians are no longer at the gates; they have entered and occupied, taking up positions in the halls of power, boardrooms of industry, centers of education, and councils of entertainment.

From inside the Church, as it was prophesied; *While his men were sleeping, his enemy came and sowed weeds* (Mathew 13:25). We should not be surprised. Paul warned us that *fierce wolves will come in among you, not sparing the flock and from among your own selves* (Acts 20:29-30). Within our walls, subversive forces of compromise and heresy plot to take down the Church. Many have already fallen.

In the meantime, churches have been warned but have not armed. Once or twice a month church attendance, paper-thin theology, anemic prayer, timid evangelism, and spare good works has left us ill-prepared for the present onslaught.

From the onset of Hitler's hostilities, Churchill called the British people to prepare for war. At the same time, he warned them that the battle would be long and hard-fought: "Now this is not the end. It is not even the beginning of the end. But it is, perhaps, the end of the beginning."

What does it look like when the Church is prepared for war? Isaiah depicts a city encircled by armed soldiers of prayer:

On your walls, O Jerusalem, I have set watchmen; all the day and all the night they shall never be silent. You who put the LORD in remembrance, take no rest, and give him no rest until he establishes Jerusalem and makes it a praise in the earth. (Isaiah 62:6-7)

In Isaiah's day, the parapet walkway on the fortified walls surrounding Jerusalem was approximately 3 kilometers around and 2.5 meters wide. If armed soldiers were placed every 10 meters, there would be 300 at their post (I pray that I would be one of these 300).

In a posture of expectant vigilance, these prayer sentries keep their eyes open in every direction. They look within the city to ensure all is safe and secure. They look to each side to ensure their fellow soldiers are ready and awake. They look outside the walls to see if danger approaches. They lift their gaze and look to God for protection.

Picture this military image for today. Any woman or man can be a watchman. Stationed in formation on the parapet, believers are ever alert in prayer. If one soldier falls asleep, the city may be breached. Every hour, one soldier after another lifts their eyes heavenward, antiphonally praising their Lord and seeking his conquering power. Night and day, the soldiers never cease to cry out to God to *make Jerusalem a praise in all the earth.*

Each watchman looks to the horizon, to the end of war, to the dispelling of darkness, and to the brightness of the rising sun of the promised day—a day when every enemy is subdued. Guarded by God, this city becomes *a house of prayer for all peoples* (Isaiah 56:7).

Early believers were watchmen, ever alert in prayer. They were *devoting themselves to prayer* (Acts 1:14, 2:42, 6:4). "Devoted" is a compound word, *proskartumenos*, combining the ideas of commitment, strength, and perseverance.

Consecrated to earnest and united prayer is how we take our station on the parapet, how we defend the Church of Christ, and how we embrace the presence and power of God.

What Today's Prayer Sentry Looks Like

Just as soldiers enter a bootcamp before active duty, every church and believer must enter a spiritual bootcamp if we are to prevail. At Prayer Current, we have dedicated more than twenty years to the task of raising up a new generation of prayer warriors. We have facilitated two-to-five-day *Prayer for the City* Bootcamps in Canada, the USA, China, Cuba, Russia, Siberia, India, and Uganda. Our purpose is to equip individual believers and churches in the essentials of Kingdom prayer.

Perhaps our most effective prayer training has been our on-site, five-day *World Street Experience* in downtown Vancouver. We hole up in a city center hotel, shelve cell phones, and meet morning and evening for prayer and interaction. Each afternoon we head out to the streets to prayer walk. One afternoon, we go to the poverty-stricken, drug-infested Downtown Eastside. Another afternoon, we prayer walk the spiritual hot zone of the West End. Two afternoons, we go out street witnessing, using prayer and spiritual conversation to engage people. In this World Street Experience, we hosted 45 leaders from Russia, India, Cuba, Canada, and the USA. On our prayer evangelism outings, we had 45 prayer conversations. We asked these seekers what we could pray for them. After we prayed for them, several were visibly moved, and a some wept.

As a staff and team, we have three scheduled days of prayer and planning each year. We pray before and during staff meetings. We have other days of prayer as needed.

We also send out regular prayer missives to hundreds of prayer supporters by text and email. This prayer cover is like deploying fighter planes that fly low to the ground to strafe the enemy front. Regular prayer communications are essential whenever we prepare for training events or during times of duress and spiritual warfare.

Victories Follow Faithful Resistance

Consider the ministry of Jesus. He was dogged by the devil from the start. With every step, he encountered the hideous strength of the evil one and his allies. Yet Jesus resisted every attack, and the gospel advanced in power.

At the outset of his ministry, Jesus fasted for 40 days and withstood Satan in the wilderness (Luke 4:13). From that day forward, Jesus' miraculous deliverance ministry exploded.

They brought to him all who were sick or oppressed by demons. … And he healed many who were sick with various diseases, and cast out many demons. And he would not permit the demons to speak, because they knew him. (Mark 1:32, 34)

He cast out the spirits with a word. (Matthew 8:16)

The same sequence of resistance and advance is repeated in the narrative of the early Church. From Jerusalem to Judea and then to Samaria, in less than a decade the Church had multiplied through three countries.

So the church throughout all Judea and Galilee and Samaria had peace and was being built up. And walking in the fear of the Lord and comfort of the Holy Spirit, it multiplied. (Acts 9:31)

In the train of this triumphal procession were thousands of conversions, hundreds of house churches, believers gladly sharing possessions, and worship, *continually filled with awe.* (Acts 2:43, 4:31-35).

Even unbelievers were struck by the manifest power of the early church: *Fear came upon the whole church and upon all who* heard these things ... the people held them in high esteem (Acts 5:11,13). Christians were salt and light; a counterculture within the culture; a city of God within the city of man.

Yet, every inch of enemy territory had to be hard earned. With every advance, the early church met fierce opposition.

They faced intimidation, interrogation, beatings, imprisonment, and martyrdom.

> *Greatly annoyed because they were teaching the people and proclaiming in Jesus the resurrection from the dead ... the rulers and elders and scribes gathered together in Jerusalem ... "By what power and what name did you do this?" ... In order that it may spread no further among the people ... they charged them not to speak or teach at all in the name of Jesus.* (Acts 4:2, 5, 7, 17-18)

The disciples take a courageous stand, saying *We cannot but speak of the things we have seen and heard* (Acts 4:20). Immediately, they bring out the heavy artillery of prayer.

> *They lifted their voices together [in prayer] ... The kings of the earth set themselves, and the rulers were gathered together, against the Lord and against his Anointed, for truly in this city there were gathered together against your holy servant Jesus, both Herod and Pontius Pilate along with the Gentiles and the peoples of Israel ...* (Acts 4:24, 26-27)

The results were astonishing. God answered with a second Pentecost.

> *And when they had prayed, the place where they were gathered together was shaken, and they were all filled with the Holy Spirit and all spoke the word of God with boldness.* (Acts 4:31)

Before long, the apostles were arrested again and imprisoned for defying the court order: *Filled with jealousy [the high priests and the Sadducees] arrested the apostles and put them in prison* (Acts 5:17-18). But the Holy Spirit had other plans.

> *But during the night an angel of the Lord opened the prison doors and brought them out, and said, "Go ... speak to the people all the words of this Life." And when they heard this, they entered the temple at daybreak and began to teach.* (Acts 5:19-21)

This jailbreak enraged the ruling council and when they called in the apostles, *they beat them and charged them not to speak in the name of Jesus before letting them go* (Acts 5:40). Yet the gospel continued to multiply and increase: *Every day, in the temple and from house to house, they did not cease teaching and preaching that the Christ is Jesus* (Acts 5:42).

Shortly after hostility turned to murder when Stephen confronted the religious authorities and exposed their hypocrisy: *You stiff-necked people ... you always resist the Holy Spirit ... which of the prophets did your fathers not persecute?* (Acts 6:8-7:53) Even as the stones fly, Stephen prays, *Lord do not hold this sin against them* (Acts 7:60).

Once again, faithful resistance precipitates a great Kingdom expansion. After that persecution, many *were scattered throughout the regions of Judea and Samaria* (Acts 8:4; 11:19-20). The result was that *a great number of people believed and turned to the Lord* (11:21).

Faithful resistance is not retaliation. Early believers did not pray for God to harm their enemies. The Church left vindication and vengeance in the hands of the Lord. In his appointed time, God removed the enemies of the Church.

The Church also suffered internal attacks. They learned an essential lesson, "If you don't win the battles inside, you can't win the battles outside."

The first ambush was the deceit of Ananias and Sapphira, who conspired to give a false report to the apostles. Peter rebuked them—*You have not lied to man but to God* (Acts 5:4)—and the Holy Spirit executed discipline. Both Ananias and Sapphira paid the ultimate price for their collusion. After this evil was expelled, the community of believers became irresistible.

> *And great fear came upon the whole church and upon all who heard of these things. ... None of the rest dared join them, but the people held them in high esteem. And more than ever believers were added to the Lord, multitudes of both men and women.* (Acts 5:11-14)

A Spirit-filled Church advances with strong forces of exclusion as well as a powerful forces of attraction. Soon after the rapid expansion of the early Church, murmuring arose, and divisions threatened. Greek believers were unhappy with the Jewish church leaders. But the leaders did not panic—rather, they involved the people by allowing them to choose their own leaders. The Spirit healed the wounds and renewed the fellowship, so it was stronger than ever before. Unsurprisingly, conversions multiplied:

> *But we will devote ourselves to prayer and to the ministry of the word. And what they said pleased the whole gathering … The word of God continued to increase, and the number of disciples multiplied greatly in Jerusalem, and a great many priests became obedient to the faith.* (Acts 6:4-5, 7)

Three Important Observations

What can we learn from these early believers?

First, gospel advance is always met with enemy opposition.

Second, faithful resistance is blessed with divine power. When the Church takes a stand, Pentecost revival grows stronger. God sends Holy Spirit awakenings to advance the gospel. These outpourings include manifestations of power, revelations, and conversions. Enemies and opponents, inside and outside, are thwarted and shamed.

Third, a praying Church is essential for gospel advance. Consider how this little group of 120 believers moved forward with unstoppable force against unfathomable odds. When Jesus ascended, believers were outnumbered 44,000 to 1 in Palestine alone. Yet, in the face of malicious opposition from without and divisive people from within, many thousands of hearts were pierced by the gospel. In the words of Charles Spurgeon, "When God wants to do something great, he sets his people praying." We cannot expect great spiritual outpourings without united persevering prayer.

God's Promise of Conquest

It is time to return to the conquest language of the Scriptures. Consider the last book of the bible. Revelation is Gods' timely word of victory to those suffering antagonism from the world. The apocalyptic battle within its pages informs a theology of triumph. One commentary writer titles Revelation *"More than Conquerors"*; another, *"The Triumph of the Lamb."*

In Revelation, the apostle John pulls back the curtain of reality to reveal the unseen battle. Behind visible powers that oppress the Church and pillage the earth are the unseen powers, authorities, and hosts of wickedness that conspire against the Lord and his Spirit-anointed people. Our ultimate opponent is not the state and its anti-life and anti-Christian laws and decrees. Our true enemy is the dragon and his allies—the beast, the false prophet, and the world spirit, Babylon.

Revelation 2 and 3, Christ speaks to seven churches in Asia Minor, promising glorious and eternal rewards to those who take a stand and resist the devil.

To the one who conquers I will grant to eat of the tree of life. (2:7)
The one who conquers will not be hurt by the second death. (2:11)
To the one who conquers I will give ... a new name. (2:17)
I will give him the morning star. (2:28)
The one who conquers will be clothed thus in white garments
... I will confess his name before my Father. (3:5)
To the one who conquers, I will make him a pillar in the temple of my God. (3:12)
To the one who conquers, I will grant him to sit with me on my throne. (3:21)

To the victor belong the spoils.
Blessed is the man who remains steadfast under trial, for when he has stood the test he will receive the crown of life, which God has promised to those who love him. (James 1:12)

The prize of this war is to rescue lost men and women from the domain of darkness and see them transferred to the Kingdom of God's son, *in whom we have redemption, the forgiveness of sins* (Colossians 1:13-14).

HOW TO PRAY

Pray for Harvest While Under State and Public Opposition

Almighty Father, conquering Son of God, Spirit of power, we offer a prayer in your Son's name today in the hope of your Church waking to all the promises of your Word, and in hope of a great harvest of new believers here and abroad.

Lord Jesus, we pray in concert with the first believers, who, when under assault from rulers of state and Sanhedrin, cried out with a single voice and heart for you to take note of this rebellion—not that you destroy them, but that you grant your ascension power to tear down strongholds with bold proclamation. Open our eyes to the unholy alliance that has risen to oppose you, your message, and your people.

We do not pray that you destroy these enemies, but that you overpower and destroy their works. We do not ask for power to defend ourselves; we ask for power to preach and practice the gospel of your Kingdom (Acts 4:23-31). Grant us a Spirit of enlightenment and revelation that we might be filled with hope in the riches of our inheritance in the saints, and to know what is the surpassing resurrection and ascension power that inhabits us—that you might, in the eyes of a watching world, vindicate and manifest that your Church is the fullness of your saving person and power (Ephesians 1:15-23). Amen.

TESTIMONIES

The Power of Prayer Cells for Growth and Mission

The disciples asked Jesus, *teach us to pray* (Luke 11:1). As we have worked with our partners in persecuted countries like India and China, we have found that starting and multiplying prayer cells is essential for personal growth and mission advance. The Methodist movement multiplied for more than a century in the British Isles and in North America. Scholars attribute this to the resilience of the small group structure, particularly the "bands," groups of three or four people who met each week for prayer, accountability, and spiritual growth. Similar prayer cells flourished and sustained the Moravian awakening the Welsh Revival, which went global after 50,000 people were converted in Wales in 1904-05.

At Prayer Current we offer a 52-week curriculum, *Building Prayer Friendships with Jesus*, to assist in the formation of prayer cells. Partners in India helped us develop this resource and are using it to start churches everywhere.

Prayer cells do more than gather believers; they reorder hearts, turn prayer into instinct, forge community, and raise new leaders.

Kingdom Vision Replaces Crisis Fixation

"I've been a part of many prayer groups in the past that blessed me tremendously. However, our focus was praying about hardships in our lives and that of our loved ones. This focus can distort our perspectives. It can make our struggles and oppositions seem mightier than our God. (With this curriculum), we do pray about those things, but our focus is on God and his Kingdom.

Kingdom prayer gives us right thinking, unshakable hope, uncommon joy, and steady faith in believing God is who he says he is and fulfils his promises. Together in prayer, we plead to God to make his name known to all the nations and for his righteousness to reign in our hearts and in the body of Christ. Our hearts are knitted together as we seek the Holy Spirit to break our hearts for the things that breaks his."

—Steve Fults, Missionary to India, Equipping Leaders International

Accountable Community Turns Prayer into Daily Breath

"My prayer cell is like a lifeline. As well as meeting weekly, we often reach out to each other throughout the week for prayer for ourselves or to intercede for others in our communities and around the world. We have seen, firsthand, the power of prayer by having so many prayers answered. There's a real sense of power we feel when we pray as a group, knowing we are taking action where otherwise we feel defeated. These wonderful women keep me accountable and active in my prayer life and because of this, prayer has become like breathing for me. I find myself praying all day long, in all situations."

—LaToya Middleton, prayer cell member

Enduring Community Deepens Through Trial

"What makes our prayer cell unique is that all of us went through the *Prayer Revolution* training. We all speak the same language and are eager to pray Kingdom prayers for ourselves and for others. We have developed close relationships with each other and have sustained each other through hard trials. We have cried, laughed, and fought in prayer for one another, our children, and those God has put in our paths. Getting together to share and pray is like having a family reunion where we are eager to find out how we are doing and pray for one another. We are regularly in contact via email and texts between prayer meetings. I love these women."

—Axa Carnes, Prayer Cell Member

Prayer Cells Multiply Leaders, Not Just Meetings

"Because of the continuation of a weekly prayer cell, I felt prepared to start a new prayer cohort at my church to train my local body in Kingdom prayer. I believe you can never have too many prayer warriors surrounding you!"

—Caroline Adobah, Prayer Cell Leader

CONCLUSION

This book has been written so that God's people might recover Biblical spiritual warfare. In order that God's people might muster for the present conflict, we have surveyed the essentials:

In Chapters 1-6, we studied the cosmic and temporal dimensions of spiritual warfare so we can discern the spirits and know the times. With the first believers, *we can now say: We are not ignorant of his designs* (2 Corinthians 2:11).

In Chapters 5-11, we presented evidence of Satan's cunning and deceiving work in our day so we can take a stand and resist the temptations and persecutions of the enemy. In consequence, we are *not surprised at the fiery ordeal* that has come upon us (1 Peter 4:12).

In Chapters 12-15, we surveyed Biblical, historical, and contemporary testimony so we can engage and overthrow evil opponents of the gospel. *I will build my church and the gates of hell shall not prevail against it* (Matthew 16:18).

Throughout, we have asserted that our times are rife with apocalyptic signs. As prophesied, the Church is surrounded by her enemies. The furnaces of persecution are stoked seven-fold as outspoken Christians are persecuted on a global scale. Enemies of the faith proliferate and occupy seats of power and influence in every field. The powers beneath the powers that have risen to the surface in military formation.

At the same time, we see the morning sun cresting the horizon as good news is preached in every land and to every language. Evangelism campaigns conquer as indigenous workers and missionaries take captivity captive in Christ's name (Ephesians 4:8 NKJV). Day and night, soldiers of Christ risk interrogation, torture, imprisonment, and their very lives, venturing behind enemy lines. The spoils of this spiritual war are the deliverance of millions from enemy territory.

Jesus expects us to discern these signs and prepare for his imminent return: *Now when these things begin to take place, straighten up and raise your heads because your redemption is drawing near* (Luke 21:28).

Satan is a vanquished foe. *I saw Satan fall like lightning* (Luke 10:18). Yet we realize when lightning hits the ground, it starts a brushfire especially in places where there is dead undergrowth. A forest fire can cleanse but can also bring devastation.

Green forests do not ignite. For the individual believer, church, city, or nation, when the underbrush and debris of unconfessed sins accumulate and where unbelief and nominalism prevail, lightning can ignite a great fire.

We would be utterly powerless against our enemies except that we are filled and fueled by Christ's conquest over evil.

> *He has delivered us from the domain of darkness and transferred us to the kingdom of his beloved Son, in whom we have redemption, the forgiveness of sins ... He set aside [the record of debt], nailing it to the cross. He disarmed the rulers and authorities and put them to open shame, by triumphing over them in him.* (Colossians 1:13-14; 2:14-15)

Every book of the New Testament rings with confidence and certainty of our triumph in Christ—not only at the end of days but in the present era of our warfare. Listen to the words of the Captain of the Lord's host:

But take heart; I have overcome the world. (John 16:33)

I saw Satan fall like lightning from heaven. (Luke 10:18)

Now will the ruler of this world be cast out. (John 12:31)

The ruler of this world is judged. (John 16:11)

All authority in heaven and earth has been given to me ... Go therefore ... I am with you always. (Matthew 28:18-20)

Take courage in the words of the apostle as he sounds the same note of triumph:

> *How much more shall [we] reign in life.* (Romans 5:18 NKJV)

> *Thanks be to God, who in Christ always leads us in triumphal procession.* (2 Corinthians 2:14)

> *You have been filled in him, who is the head of all rule and authority.* (Colossians 2:10)

We give glory to the King of Kings. Even now and to the end of time, He rules *[his foes] with a rod of iron* (Psalm 2:9) We know that at present and in the final hour, God will *make his enemies a footstool for his feet* (Psalm 110:1).

> *But the court will sit, and [the power of the last kingdoms of the world] will be taken away and completely destroyed forever. Then the sovereignty, power and greatness of all the kingdoms under heaven will be handed over to the holy people of the Most High. His kingdom will be an everlasting kingdom, and all rulers will worship and obey him.* (Daniel 7:26-27 NIV)

A Prayer Encouragement for Everyone Who Reads This Book

Dear Father, our hearts burst with gratitude for the gift of your Son. We swell with courage and joy that you have called us to enlist in the warfare of the Lord of the Harvest, our captain and King. Though the battle be long and accompanied with many painful and malicious attacks of the enemy, we count our every loss and sorrow as gain because we have been selected, trained, and deployed in your holy service.

Great Holy Spirit, because you are the pledge and presence of our conquering Lord, we praise and thank you for being our power, guide, and comfort in every spiritual battle we fight. The tide has turned in our battles within. We can now face the enemies without because you have opened our eyes to the true nature of our conflict and the strategies of the devil. When under assault, we do not retreat, because you have given us inner assurance of our victory in Christ.

Son of God, our Redeemer and King, we embrace your commandment and commission to go forth into the nations—not only because the final victory is assured but because we love you for your proven love at the cross. In a thousand ways, each day we enjoy your close friendship and are empowered by the vision of your conquest over every enemy.

Father, Son, and Spirit, open our eyes, prepare us for the battle, and be with us as we often lose hope. Give us courage and fortitude to resist, and boldness to engage and conquer in your name and for your glory. Amen.

In all these things we are more than conquerors through him who loved us. For I am convinced that neither death nor life, neither angels nor demons, neither the present nor the future, nor any powers, neither height nor depth, nor anything else in all creation, will be able to separate us from the love of God that is in Christ Jesus our Lord. (Romans 8:37-39- NIV)

APPENDIX I

Discern + Engage

HOW TO LEAD A PRAYER-BOOK STUDY THAT BRINGS TRANSFORMATION

You've had enough of feeling the exhaustion of self-reliance and prayerlessness, hustling to make things happen out of your own effort. You're tired of the drag of stress-relief survival prayer. Your spirit is hungry for refreshing encounters with Jesus. You're ready to participate more powerfully in Christ's kingdom purpose for your life.

So, now what? How do you move from fleeting moments of prayer to a movement of prayer? How do you lead yourself and others from a posture and culture of not showing up for prayer at all, to a life of dynamic prayer that is integral to the fabric of your life and ministry?

PRAYING WITH OTHERS can be one of the best ways to break through the initial inertia. Corporate prayer can help stoke the fire of your personal prayer life by providing heightened awareness of God's presence, accountability, and discipleship.

PRACTICE paves the path for prayer power. The goal is not cerebral study of prayer. Our prayerlessness is not an information problem. Intellectual discussion about prayer and God's love for us as His children is not the same as experiencing Him from a deeply rooted place in our hearts that leads to actual transformation of our minds, hearts, and actions. Prayer bridges that eternal distance between our heads and our hearts by making room for Jesus to do the work. As Jesus said, "You will know the truth, and the truth will set you free." (John 8:32)

Discern + Engage

Commit to finding at least one other person to pray through this book together to begin harnessing the power of prayer first hand. Offer up a simple prayer, "Jesus, thank You for the gift of prayer, which You've given through the price of Your own sacrifice. Thank You that You are the prize. I know You desire for me to know You more deeply through prayer and to bring others to prayer so they can encounter You too. Will You show me who in my life currently I might ask to join me? Is there someone new that I have yet to meet? Bring our paths to cross and open the door for us to pray together so that Your kingdom may come more fully in our lives and in the worlds You've placed us in. In Your name, Amen."

Facilitate your prayer time in a way that guards the priority of practicing prayer.

This is true in all contexts, whether you pray with a friend one on one, or with your family, small group, or leadership team. Invite people to join you for a prayer group (rather than calling it a book study). Set a tone of coming to meet with Jesus in a direct experiential way. Create a space of trust and confidentiality so people can feel free to open themselves to the group and ultimately to God in a vulnerable way.

Set the path for dynamic, fresh kingdom prayer by keeping the ball moving.

· Keep the prayer clusters short and groups of people small (if your group is large)

· Break people into smaller groups of 2-4 so that everyone gets ample opportunity to pray and interact, as this is where they wrestle with and apply the truths to their own lives.

Encourage participants to pray practicing the ABCs of corporate prayer :

Audible • Brief • Christ-centered

· Pray **Audibly** so others can pray in agreement with you.

· Pray **Brief prayers** (you can pray more than once) to keep the ball moving. This is assuring for newbies, and sets of the boundary for long sermonizing prayers.

· Pray **Christ-centered,** Conversational prayers in Concert with one another.

═══ **"Prayer is spiritual warfare. Be alert and expect resistance."** ═══

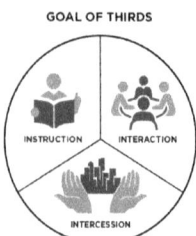

GOAL OF THIRDS

PRACTICE THE GOAL OF THIRDS: 1/3 instruction, 1/3 interaction, 1/3 intercession.

Plan to intersperse the prayer throughout the gathering, not just leaving it until the end, as it will get squeezed out.

Discern + Engage

THE FOLLOWING IS A SAMPLE TIMELINE FOR A 75-MINUTE GATHERING:

Homework	Have everyone read the reading selection ahead of time. Have each person choose one paragraph of choose one paragraph that they found insightful and draft one paragraph of prayer in response.
5 minutes	To open your gathering, have one person open in prayer and summarize the chapter.
10 minutes	Divide people into groups of 3-4. Have each person share their one insight with their group and engage in a discussion together.
10 minutes	Remaining in their small groups, have an open time of praying in response of prayer to what came up during the discussion.
10 minutes	Back in the large group, the key leader shares a prophetic insight and immediate application/implication to the current cultural context. Leader provides 2 prayer prompts. Have people pray for the church, mission, and city.
10 minutes	Divide into small groups, have an open time of praying in response, guided by the prayer prompts.
10 minutes	Break people into groups of 2 for a time of application and peer coaching. Each person discusses with their partner 1-2 practical ways they can bring prayer into their area of leadership. Be sure to cue them to pray for one another by name.
10 minutes	Gather in the large group. Provide opportunity for people who would like to share their practical takeaway or application with the whole group, which may inspire others with new ideas.
10 minutes	Share answers to prayer and thanksgiving.

Prepare in prayer. Stand guard in prayer. Advance in prayer.
Prayer is spiritual warfare. Be alert and expect resistance.

• Praying for the Holy Spirit to transform hearts and habits and making room for people to engage first hand is more essential than having the best teaching or leadership skills.

• Pray for each participant and session to be rich in prayer and fellowship with Jesus.

• Pray for your heart to be soft and surrendered to the agenda and guidance of the Holy Spirit.

• Build a "prayer-backup team" and regularly solicit coverage from them.

• Praise and rejoice in the answers and presence of Jesus that comes.

For further resources and support on growing a life and mission in prayer, visit prayercurrent.com.

3

Recommended Resources For Further Study

Works on Spiritual Warfare

Bunyan, John. *The Pilgrim's Progress*. First published 1678. Various editions available.
The classic allegory on the Christian journey to the Celestial City—second only to the Bible in copies distributed.

Ellul, Jacques. *The Meaning of the City*. Grand Rapids, MI: Eerdmans, 1970.
A prophetic analysis of the spiritual processes that lead to cities built on human autonomy.

Ferrer, Ada. *Cuba: An American History*. New York: Scribner, 2021.

Hurtado, Larry W. *Destroyer of the Gods: Early Christian Distinctiveness in the Roman World*. Waco, TX: Baylor University Press, 2017.
A history of the early Church's struggles and victories within an idolatrous culture.

Johnson, Dennis E. *Triumph of the Lamb: A Commentary on Revelation*. Phillipsburg, NJ: P&R Publishing, 2001.
A fair and detailed treatment of various end-times interpretations.

Jones, Peter. *The Gnostic Empire Strikes Back*. Phillipsburg, NJ: P&R Publishing, 1992.
A historical analysis of the pagan roots of New Age religion.

Lewis, C. S. *Perelandra*. Originally published 1943. New York: Simon & Schuster, 2011.
A theological imagination: What if Satan visited a new pristine world?

Lewis, C. S. *That Hideous Strength*. New York: Simon & Schuster, 2011.
Lewis's portrayal of diabolic influences in higher education.

Lewis, Nathan. "Angels and Demons." Four sermons. Accessed at www.prayercurrent.com.
A thorough biblical overview of the influence of angels and demons.

McIntyre, David M. *The Hidden Life of Prayer*. London: Morgan & Scott, 1906.
A survey of the "closet prayer" lives of spiritual leaders.

Orr, J. Edwin. *The Re-study of Revival and Revivalism*. Wheaton, IL: International Awakening Press, 2000.

Rhodes, Ron. *Angels Among Us*. Nashville: Thomas Nelson, 2008.

Steger, Manfred B. *Globalization: A Very Short Introduction*. 6th ed. Oxford: Oxford University Press, 2023.

Thornbury, John. *Five Pioneer Missionaries*. Edinburgh: Banner of Truth, 1965.
Demonstrates that missionary endeavor is frontline spiritual warfare.

The Trinity Hymnal. Phillipsburg, NJ: Great Commission Publications, 1961.
See especially hymns 477–490 on warfare, ascension, and exaltation.

Wang, Yi, et al. *Faithful Disobedience: Writings on Church and State from a Chinese House Church Movement*. Edited by Hannah Nation. Downers Grove, IL: IVP, 2022.

Zacharias, Bryan. *The Embattled Christian*. Edinburgh: Banner of Truth, 1995.
A primer on spiritual warfare drawing from Puritan perspectives.

Strategic Background Reading

Bevins, Winfield. *The Marks of a Movement: What the Bible Reveals About the Essential Patterns of God's Kingdom*. Grand Rapids, MI: Zondervan, 2019.
An analysis of the critical factors in a sustained gospel awakening.

Ferry, Luc. *A Brief History of Thought: A Philosophical Guide to Living*. New York: Harper Perennial, 2011.
A thoughtful survey of Western philosophy.

Flew, Antony. *There Is a God: How the World's Most Notorious Atheist Changed His Mind*. New York: HarperCollins, 2008.
A former atheist drinks his own medicine and becomes a theist.

Haidt, Jonathan. *The Anxious Generation: How the Great Rewiring of Childhood Is Causing an Epidemic of Mental Illness*. New York: Penguin Press, 2024.
An essential investigation into the collapse of youth mental health—and a plan for a healthier, freer childhood.

Nation, Hannah. "Chinese Lessons in Apologetics." Comment, December 2023. https://comment.org/chinese-lessons-in-apologetics/.

Smith, James K. A. *How (Not) to Be Secular: Reading Charles Taylor.* Grand Rapids, MI: Eerdmans, 2014.

A layman's guide to Charles Taylor's *A Secular Age.*

Smed, John. *Prayer Revolution: Rebuilding Church and City through* Prayer. Chicago: Moody Publishers, 2020.
A scriptural and historical overview of the place of prayer in revivals.

Wilberforce, William. *Real Christianity.* Minneapolis, MN: Bethany House, 2006.
A portrait of day-to-day spiritual battle in the public sphere.

About Prayer Current

Prayer Current equips church and mission leaders to multiply praying leaders who build houses and movements of prayer.

Forged in the furnace of 25 years of urban church planting, Prayer Current has designed **dynamic prayer training resources and course curriculum** to equip thousands of leaders to **systemically build cultures of missional prayer discipleship** within their ministries—revolutionizing vision, building resilience, and restoring joy in the Spirit.

Since 2000, Prayer Current's passion has been to empower church and mission leaders in the global church and ministry networks. Field-tested training and resources lay a foundation for sustainable growth, deep transformation, and harvest fruit by casting vision through **biblical instruction, small group interaction, practical tools, and hands-on prayer experiences**. Through **kingdom-centered prayer**, leaders and their people discover renewed vision, resurrection power, deeper love for God, the Church, and the nations, and an increased capacity to grow ministries in maturity.

To explore additional resources and training, visit the Prayer Current website at www.prayercurrent.com

www.ingramcontent.com/pod-product-compliance
Lightning Source LLC
Chambersburg PA
CBHW060834190426
43197CB00039B/2593